CAMBRIDGE Professional English

for work and life
English 365

Personal Study Book 1
with Audio CD

T0349514

Bob Dignen Steve Flinders Simon Sweeney

CAMBRIDGE
UNIVERSITY PRESS

CAMBRIDGE UNIVERSITY PRESS
Cambridge, New York, Melbourne, Madrid, Cape Town,
Singapore, São Paulo, Delhi, Tokyo, Mexico City

Cambridge University Press
The Edinburgh Building, Cambridge CB2 8RU, UK

www.cambridge.org
Information on this title: www.cambridge.org/9780521753647

First published 2004
10th printing 2011

Printed in the United Kingdom at the University Press, Cambridge

A catalogue record for this publication is available from the British Library

ISBN 978-0-521-75364-7 Personal Study Book 1 with Audio CD
ISBN 978-0-521-75362-3 Student's Book 1
ISBN 978-0-521-75363-0 Teacher's Book 1
ISBN 978-0-521-75365-4 Student's Book 1 Audio Cassette Set
ISBN 978-0-521-75366-1 Student's Book 1 Audio CD Set

Contents

Personal Study Book

Personal Study Book Audio CD

English365

Personal Study Book 1

Introduction

Welcome to the *English365* Personal Study Book 1. This book and Audio CD are to help you to practise and learn the English you need for work and for your free time. There are two parts to the book:

Personal Study Book

This **Introduction** tells you about the organisation of the book and CD.

Better language learning gives you ideas about what good learners do to learn more English.

Language for language learning gives you words you must understand – like 'noun', 'verb' and 'check' – for your work in the classroom and for homework.

The **Practice exercises** give you one page of self-study exercises for each unit (1–30) in the *English365* Student's Book 1. You can do one page of exercises after each classroom lesson:
- exercises for type 1 units (Units 1, 4, 7, 10, 13, 16, 19, 22, 25 and 28) practise grammar and sometimes pronunciation
- exercises for type 2 units (Units 2, 5, 8, 11, 14, 17, 20, 23, 26 and 29) practise vocabulary and skills you need for your work
- exercises for type 3 units (Units 3, 6, 9, 12, 15, 18, 21, 24, 27 and 30) practise the English you need for everyday situations and general vocabulary.

Personal Study Book Audio CD

The **Listening units** are to give you practice in some of the basics of English like numbers, spelling, etc. You can listen to the exercises on the CD, write your answers in the book and then check your answers in the Answer key.

The Audio CD also contains work from the *English365* Student's Book 1 which you can practise on your own:
- **Pronunciation** (type 1 units) and
- **Social English dialogues** (type 3 units).

The Tapescript for these is at the back of this book. See page 64 for the contents of the CD.

Better language learning

Working with your teacher and with other learners in the classroom is important for your English. It is also important for you to work on your own. This book and the Audio CD are to help you work between lessons and to remember the work you do with your teacher. Your objective is to learn English and also to learn how to learn English better. If you learn to be a better learner, you will learn more and you will learn faster. Here are ten steps to help you to learn better and faster.

1 Think about **why** you want to learn.
2 Think about **how important** it is to learn English. If it is important for you and your job, you will give it a lot of time. But remember: it is difficult to learn a language well without classroom lessons <u>and</u> practice outside the classroom.
3 Decide **how much time** you can give to your English. You can learn a lot in five or ten minutes per day. Little and often is best.
4 Think about **what** you want to learn. Have an objective for each day, each week and each month.
5 Think about **how** you learn. For example, do you like to hear new language or to write it down or to see it on the page? Do the things that are best for you.
6 **Plan** your work for the day, for the week and for the month to come.
7 **Reward** yourself. Give yourself a present when you reach a goal.
8 **Think about** yourself **learning well** and speaking English well. This 'mental modelling' can be good for your learning.
9 Keep **a diary**. Good learners think about what and how they are learning. Write about:
   • what you study
   • when you study
   • how you feel about your study.

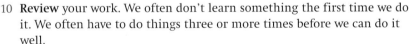

Keep a diary.

10 **Review** your work. We often don't learn something the first time we do it. We often have to do things three or more times before we can do it well.

Use pages 8–10 to write your own learning plan. You may also discuss some of these questions with your teacher and with the other people in your class. Thinking about the questions before you talk about them is also good for your learning!

PLAN
what you are going to learn.
Have clear goals.

PRACTISE
what you are learning.

REVIEW
what you have learnt.

For more ideas about improving the way you learn, look at *Learning to Learn English* by Gail Ellis and Barbara Sinclair, published by Cambridge University Press.

Better language learning notes

Write your own notes to help you learn English better and faster. It's a good idea to write your answers in pencil. Your answers to some questions may change as your learning gets better.

It's not necessary to answer all the questions. But answering some of them – even just one or two of them – will help you think about your learning and help you to be a better learner. Choose the questions you think are the most useful and work on them.

Step 1: Why do I want to learn English?

1 ....

2 ....

3 ....

Notes:

Step 2: How important is it for me to learn English?

Learning English is:

Very important   ▨   Not very important ▨

Quite important ▨   Not at all important ▨

Notes:

Step 3: How much time can I give to my English?
I can give:

5 minutes a day ▨   30 minutes a day ▨
10 minutes a day ▨   45 minutes a day ▨
15 minutes a day ▨   60 minutes a day ▨
20 minutes a day ▨

> *Notes:*

Step 4: What do I want to learn?
Write in pencil and use an eraser so that you can change your objectives each day/week/month.
My objectives for today are:
1 ....
2 ....
3 ....
My objectives for this week are:
1 ....
2 ....
3 ....
My objectives for this month are:
1 ....
2 ....
3 ....

> *Notes:*

Step 5: How do I learn?
When I am learning English I like to: ....
When I am learning English I don't much like to: ....

> *Notes:*

Step 6: What is my plan for my learning?
Today I plan to do these activities: ....
This week I plan to do these activities: ....
This month I plan do these activities: ....

> *Notes:*

Step 7: How will I reward myself if I do everything in my plan?
My reward for this week's work will be:...
My reward for this month's work will be: ....

Notes:

Step 8: How do I think of myself speaking English well?
Think about yourself speaking English well. Write down:
- what you are talking about:...
- who you are talking to: ....
- where you are talking:...
- the time of day: ....
What do you need to do to make this picture come true?

Notes:

Step 9: How do I keep a diary of my learning?
Use this checklist:
- Do I have a notebook to write my diary in? ....
- How shall I organise my diary?..
- Will I write in it every day/week/month?...................................
- What shall I write in it? ....

Notes:

Step 10: Do I review my work?
Do I review my work?...
What should I review? ....
How often should I review?..

Notes:

Language for language learning

These are words we use to talk about English. You meet them all in *English365*. They will help you understand the work you do in the classroom and for homework. Use your dictionary to write your own translation of words you don't know.

Answer (verb/noun)
Verb: To speak back to someone who asks you a question.
Noun: What you say to someone who asks you a question.

Arrow (noun)
A symbol (→) to show a direction.

Ask (verb)
To say something to someone as a question which you want them to answer.

Below (preposition)
Something is below something else when it is under it on the page.

Category (noun)
A group of things of a similar type.

Check (verb)
To look at something to make sure that it is correct or the way it should be.

Choose (verb)
To decide which thing you want.

Communication (noun)
Exchange of information with other people by writing, speaking, etc. For example, in a meeting or on the telephone.

Compare (verb)
To look at the ways in which two people or things are different or similar.

Comparative (adjective)
The form of an adjective or adverb used to show that someone or something has more of something than someone or something else. For example, 'better' is the comparative of 'good' and 'smaller' is the comparative of 'small'.

Comparison (noun)
When you compare two or more people or things.

Complete (verb)
To give or add the last part to something to make it whole.

Consonant (noun)
A letter of the alphabet that is not a vowel: 'B' and 'C' are consonants, 'A' and 'E' are not consonants.

Continue (verb)
To go on doing something.

Correct (adjective)
Accurate; with no mistakes.

Countable (adjective/noun)
A noun with a singular and plural form. For example, 'girl/girls'.

Cover (verb)
To put something over something else, in order to hide it. For example, you can cover one page of your book with your hand.

Describe (verb)
To say what someone or something is like.

Description (noun)
Something that tells you what someone or something is like.

Dialogue (noun)
A conversation between two or more people.

Dictionary (noun)
A book that contains a list of words in alphabetical order with their meanings explained.

Expression (noun)
A group of words which often go together or a phrase with a special meaning.

Grammar (noun)
The way you combine words and change their form and position in a sentence, or the rules or study of this.

Heading (noun)
Words at the top of a piece of writing that tell you what it is about.

Irregular (adjective)
Something which does not follow a general grammar rule. The opposite of 'irregular' is 'regular'. For example, 'go → went → gone' is an irregular verb.

Link (verb)
To make a connection between two or more things.

Listen (verb)
To give attention to someone or something in order to hear them. For example, you can listen to music on a CD or to a programme on the radio.

Match (verb)
If two things match, they are the same colour or type.

Mistake (noun)
When you make a mistake, you do or say something wrong. 'She am Chinese' is a mistake in English. 'She is Chinese' is correct.

Negative (adjective)
A word or phrase which expresses the meaning 'no' or 'not'. 'She is not Chinese' is the negative form of the sentence 'She is Chinese.'

Noun (noun)
A word that refers to a person, place, object, event, substance, idea, feeling or quality. For example, the words 'teacher', 'book' and 'town' are nouns.

Opposite (noun)
Completely different from another person or thing. For example, the opposite of 'good' is 'bad'.

Positive (adjective)
The opposite of negative. For example, 'She is Chinese' is the positive form of the negative sentence 'She is not Chinese.'

Preposition (noun)
A word or group of words that is used before a noun or pronoun to show place, direction, time, etc. 'In', 'at', 'on' and 'under' are all prepositions.

Present (verb)
To give information in a formal way. For example, you can make a short presentation about the organisation you work for to the rest of your class.

Pronunciation (verb)
The way that you make the sounds of letters and words.

Question (noun)
A sentence or phrase that asks you for information. 'Is he busy?', 'What time is it?', and 'Where are you going?' are all questions.

Regular (adjective)
Following the usual rules or patterns in grammar. For example, 'present → presented → presented' is a regular verb. The opposite of 'regular' is 'irregular'.

Remember (verb)
If you remember a fact or something from the past, you keep it in your mind, or bring it back into your mind. The opposite of 'remember' is 'forget'.

Reply (verb/noun)
Verb: To answer.
Noun: An answer.

Role (noun)
Actors play roles in films. Students play the roles of different people in role-play exercises in the language classroom. For example, you can play the role of the head of the department in a meeting.

Rule (noun)
A rule tells us something about how a system, for example a grammar system, works. For example, the rule about making questions with the verb 'to be' in English tells us to change the order of the subject and the verb: 'He is happy → Is he happy?'

Schwa (noun)
The schwa is the pronunciation symbol /ə/ as in 'teacher' → /tiːtʃə/ and 'opposite' → /ɒpəzɪt/.

Sentence (noun)
A group of words, usually containing a verb, which expresses a complete idea. Sentences begin with a capital letter and finish with a full stop (.), a question mark (?) or an exclamation mark (!).

Skill (noun)
To have a skill is to do an activity or a job well. In language learning, there are four main skills: speaking, listening, reading and writing. You also need to learn communication skills for your work like telephoning and writing emails.

Stress (verb/noun)
When you say one part of a word more strongly. For example, 'important' has three syllables and when you pronounce it, you stress the second syllable.

Strong (adjective)
The opposite of 'weak'. You give the second syllable in 'important' strong stress and you give the other two syllables weak stress.

Superlative (noun)
The form of an adjective or adverb that is used to show that someone or something has more of something than anyone or anything else. For example, 'best' is the superlative of 'good' and 'slowest' is the superlative of 'slow'.

Syllable (noun)
A word or part of a word that has one vowel sound. For example, 'important' has three syllables.

Tense (noun)
The form of a verb which shows the time when an action happened. For example, 'I sing' is in the present tense and 'I sang' is in the past tense.

Uncountable (adjective/noun)
A noun which does not have a plural form and cannot be used with 'a' or 'one'. For example, 'music' and 'furniture' are uncountable nouns.

Underline (verb)
To draw a line under a word or sentence. In this sentence, the word 'underline' is underlined.

Verb (noun)
'Arrive', 'make', 'be', and 'feel' are all examples of verbs.

Vocabulary (noun)
The words of a language. Your vocabulary is all the words you know in a particular language.

Vowel (noun)
A speech sound that you make with your lips and teeth open, shown in English by the letters 'a', 'e', 'i', 'o' and 'u'.

Weak (adjective)
The opposite of 'strong'. You give the third syllable in 'presentation' strong stress and you give the other three syllables weak stress.

Practice exercises

Introductions: Meeting people 1

1 There are different ways of saying the same thing when we meet.
Which sentences and questions in 1–10 say the same thing as those
in a–j?

1 Hello.	a I'm with . . .
2 My name is . . .	b I come from . . .
3 Pleased to meet you.	c Who do you work for?
4 What do you do?	d Hi.
5 I'm a . . .	e Where are you based?
6 What's the name of your company?	f Where do you come from?
7 I work for . . .	g What's your job?
8 Where are you from?	h I'm . . .
9 I'm from . . .	i My job is to . . .
10 Where do you work?	j Nice to meet you.

Grammar: Present simple – Meeting people 2

2 Look at this conversation. The underlined words are wrong. Can you
correct them?

DAVID: Hello. Nice to meet you. I (1) are David Shaw.

RACHEL: Hello, David. My name's Rachel. (2) Are you work here?

DAVID: No, I work (3) at Paris.

RACHEL: Really. That's nice. Who do you (4) working for?

DAVID: I (5) working for a big chocolate company in France.

RACHEL: Chocolate! I love chocolate! And what (6) does you do?

DAVID: I (7) is an engineer. And how about you? What (8) does you
(9) doing?

RACHEL: Me? I (10) working in a bank, here in London. (11) Does you
(12) likes your job?

DAVID: Yes, I (13) am liking my job but I (14) doesn't (15) likes chocolate!

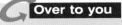 **Over to you**

Write a conversation between two professional people meeting for the first time.

Unit 2

Work vocabulary: Job responsibilities

1 When Gordon talks about his job, he says everything twice to make it seem more important. Which sentences in a–d mean the same as those in 1–4?

1 I'm in charge of a big department.
2 I work with a group of managers from ten different countries.
3 I'm the head of a big group of workers.
4 I meet clients every day.

a I manage a lot of people.
b I see customers five times a week.
c I'm part of an international management team.
d I'm responsible for a big part of the company.

2 Complete these sentences with the right preposition.

1 I work .... a company called PassGo.

2 I work .... the sales department.

3 I work .... people from all over the world.

4 I work .... London.

I'm really importa

I'm very important.

Professional communication: Telephoning phrases

3 Put the sentences in the right order in this phone conversation. The first one has been done for you.

☐ Good morning, Ms Wagner, this is Joe Stoppard. We met last week.
☐ I'm fine. What can I do for you?
☐ Goodbye.
☐ Hello. Could I speak to Sandra Wagner, please?
☐ Fine thanks, and you?
1 Good morning. CDA.
☐ Sure. I have your address. I'll send it today.
☐ One moment, please.
☐ Thanks a lot. Goodbye.
☐ Oh hello, Mr Stoppard. Yes, I remember. How are you?
☐ I'd like your brochure. Can you send me one?
☐ Hello. Sandra Wagner.

Over to you

Make sentences about your job using the same expressions as in exercise 1.

16 Personal Study Book

General communication: Social talk at the office

1 Put the words in the right order in each sentence.

1 how hello you are?
2 some for ready lunch?
3 where want eat you to do?
4 Friday thank it's goodness.
5 do any for the you have weekend plans?
6 I'm to going brother my visit.
7 next you week see.
8 weekend a have good.

General vocabulary: Free-time activities

2 Match the pictures with the free-time and housework activities.

playing the guitar   ironing   skiing   cinema   going on holiday with friends

swimming   playing the piano   cleaning   theatre   inviting friends to dinner

3 Which activities go in which group?

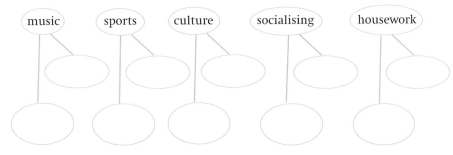

music   sports   culture   socialising   housework

Over to you

Make your own sentences for each activity with these words:

I love . . .   I like . . .   I'm interested in . . .   I quite like . . .   I don't like . . .
I hate . . .   I absolutely hate . . .

Unit 4

Grammar: Present simple – work routines

1 This is Maria's daily routine. Choose the right verb for each space, and put it into the correct form. You can use some verbs more than once.

6.30   She .... up.

7.00   She .... breakfast.

7.30   She .... home.

8.00   She .... work.

8.10   She .... a cup of coffee.

9.00   She .... her emails.

9.30   She .... on her computer.

11.00 She .... a meeting with a client.

12.00 She .... lunch.

13.30 She .... some telephone calls.

17.00 She .... work.

17.30 She .... home.

19.00 She .... dinner.

20.00 She .... TV.

23.30 She .... to bed.

make
finish
go
leave
work
check
start
get
watch
have

Grammar: Frequency expressions

2 Kenneth is a busy man. Number these sentences about his life from most often (1) to least often (11).

    He doesn't go to the Far East very often.
    He occasionally has lunch in the company restaurant.
    He has a meeting with his boss every two weeks.
    He visits the main factory in Birmingham once a month.
    He sometimes goes to Spain in the summer.
    He usually plays tennis at the weekend.
    He never goes to meetings before 8.30 in the morning.
    He often gets phone calls from his main customer in the evenings.
    He rarely reads a book.
    He always reads his favourite magazine on Fridays.
    He takes his children to school every day.

Over to you

1 Describe your daily routine, e.g. *I get up at 6.00*. Is your routine the same as Maria's? What's different? 2 Write sentences about something you often do, ·
sometimes do, occasionally do, rarely do, and that you never do.

Kenneth usually plays tennis at the weekend.

Work vocabulary: Organisations

1 There is one extra word in each of these typical company questions. Which word is incorrect in each question?
1 Who do you company work for?
2 What is the main activity of for your company?
3 Where is the location headquarters of the company?
4 What is the turnover of finance your company?
5 How much many people work for your company?

2 Put the words in brackets in the right places in these sentences. Use the correct form of the verb.
1 Daniel is a .... He has a small .... in Berlin. Companies .... him on financial and management questions. (consult – consultant – consultancy)
2 I am a personnel .... I'm very interested in people .... I .... a team of ten people. (management – manager – manage)
3 Our business is very .... We have to .... with a lot of other companies. Our main .... are in the USA and Japan. (compete – competitors – competitive)
4 We .... about 3,000 people. About 60% of the .... are women. We are the biggest .... in the town. (employees – employer – employ)

Professional communication: Taking phone messages

3 Put the words in the right order in each sentence.
1 a take I message can?
2 the today in he's office not.
3 next away she's Monday until.
4 I'll it she make gets sure.
5 back him could to me you ask call?
6 that you could repeat?
7 will later back please you call?
8 I your can number have?

> I'll give her the message when she comes in.

4 Spelling Say these letters aloud to yourself and then decide which one does not fit in each group. (For practice in saying the alphabet, see the Audio CD section, page 66.)

1 A – H – N   3 M – R – S   5 G – T – O
2 D – I – P   4 Y – J – K   6 Q – V – U

 Over to you Can you answer the five questions in exercise 1?

Unit 6

General communication: Shopping

1 Here are some typical sentences for shopping. Use one word from the box to complete each sentence.

1 Where can I .... a film for my camera?
2 What time does the shop .... ?
3 Where is the .... supermarket, please?
4 Do you .... women's shoes?
5 How .... is this, please?
6 Can I .... it on?
7 Do you have one in a .... size?
8 This is fine. I'll .... it.
9 Can I .... by credit card?
10 Can I have a .... , please?

| receipt |
| take |
| sell |
| open |
| pay |
| nearest |
| larger |
| try |
| buy |
| much |

General vocabulary: Where you live

2 Choose the right words from the box to complete the sentences. You can use some of them more than once.

1 Lorenza Tims lives .... York.
2 York is a historic city .... the north of England.
3 It is about 40 kilometres .... the sea.
4 The nearest town .... the coast is Scarborough.
5 Scarborough is .... from York.
6 She lives .... the city centre, 20 minutes' walk from the cathedral.
7 Her house is .... a quiet street near the main road to Leeds.
8 York is about 30 kilometres .... of Leeds.

| from |
| in |
| north-east |
| not far |
| near |
| on |

○ Scarborough

3 Think of a verb to finish each of these sentences about travelling to work. Remember to use the right form of the verb.

A: How do you .... to work?   ○ York
B: I .... the bus.   ○ Leeds
A: Where do you .... it?
B: I .... to the supermarket. A bus .... from there every ten minutes.

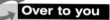

Over to you

Write sentences: 1 about the place where you live: where is it? where is it near? etc.
2 about how you travel to work.

Grammar: *There is* and *there are*; *some* and *any*; countable and uncountable nouns

1 Complete the sentences with There's or There are.

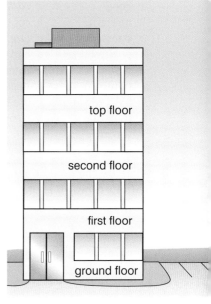

1 .... two training rooms on the first floor.

2 .... a reception area on the ground floor.

3 .... some open plan offices on the second floor.

4 .... a lot of computer equipment on the first floor.

5 .... a lot of offices on the top floor.

6 .... a large car park next to the building.

7 .... the latest company news on the computer in reception.

8 .... no swimming pool.

2 Underline the correct choice in each of these sentences.

1 Did you hear *a | the* news about the president?

2 Did you get *an | any* information about prices?

3 I gave him *some | a* money but he said it wasn't enough.

4 I think we need *some | any* time to solve this problem.

5 He lost *a | some* suitcase at the airport.

6 He lost *some | a* luggage at the airport.

7 We have *a | some* problem with the computer again.

8 He has *a | some* good job but at the moment he doesn't have *a | any* work to do.

 **Over to you**

Describe the place where you work using *There is* and *There are*.

Unit 8

Work vocabulary: Describing people

1 Match the opposites of these words:

				Carla is very stressed.
1	good	a	confident	
2	modern	b	cold	
3	stressed	c	late	
4	positive	d	bad	
5	shy	e	interesting	
6	polite	f	negative	
7	hard-working	g	old-fashioned	
8	punctual	h	rude	
9	warm	i	relaxed	
10	boring	j	lazy	

2 What are the direct opposites of these words? Use un- (three times), in- (four times), im- (once) or dis- (twice).

efficient   popular   organised   direct   patient   tidy
reliable   sensitive   honest   experienced

Professional communication: Meeting a visitor at the airport

3 Choose one word from the box to complete each sentence.

weather	right	raining	How	work	awful	trip	help
food	Thanks	Excuse	bags	Pleased	Welcome	sleep	

MAY: .... me. Are you Mr Ducroix from Lambert Holdings?

PIERRE: Yes, that's .... Pierre Ducroix. And are you May Lester?

MAY: Yes. .... to meet you.

PIERRE: Nice to meet you. .... for coming to meet me.

MAY: Not at all. It's only 20 minutes from the office. .... to Edinburgh. .... was the ....?

PIERRE: It was good. I had a .... and did some .... , and the .... was OK.

MAY: And how's the .... in Paris?

PIERRE: It's .... It doesn't stop ....!

MAY: Oh dear. Well, it's good here. Can I .... you with your ....?

PIERRE: No thanks, I'm OK.

MAY: Good. Well, the car's in the car park just over there . . .

Over to you

Which words in exercise **1** do you think are positive and which are negative?

General communication: Getting around

1 **Which pairs of words go together?**

a cab · a bus · the underground · a boat

the subway · a coach · a taxi · a ferry

2 **Look at what visitors say as they travel round a city. Match the questions and answers.**

1 Can you tell me where the coach station is?

2 Can I buy a ticket on the bus?

3 Two singles to the city centre, please.

4 What time is the next boat down the river?

5 Thanks for the ride. Keep the change.

6 Can I have a receipt, please?

7 Does this bus go to the cathedral?

8 What's the best way to get to the National Museum?

a No, you have to get one at the ticket office over there.

b Yes, here you are.

c It's at 3 o'clock – in about 20 minutes.

d No, it only goes to the river. You want a number 37.

e Thank you, madam. Have a nice day.

f You should take a tram from the main square.

g It's straight down this road on the left.

h That's €3, please.

General vocabulary: Where you live

3 **Match the second part of each sentence (a–j) with the right first part (1–10) to make ten complete sentences.**

1 The people are (*good thing*)

2 The service in shops and hotels is (*bad thing*)

3 The public transport system is (*good thing*)

4 The cinemas are (*bad thing*)

5 The food is (*good thing*)

6 The traffic is (*bad thing*)

7 The nightlife is (*good thing*)

8 Crime is (*bad thing*)

9 The buildings are (*good thing*)

10 The weather is (*bad thing*)

a very tasty.

b very wet.

c very well-designed.

d going up.

e very exciting.

f very poor.

g very fast.

h very smoky.

i very noisy.

j very friendly.

Over to you

Make sentences about the place where you live. Describe the weather, the people, the service, etc. as in exercise **3**.

Unit 10

Grammar: Comparatives

1 Write the correct form of a word from the box to complete each sentence.

1 Tokyo is .... to Beijing than Washington.
2 Washington is .... from Tokyo than Beijing.
3 Climbing is a .... sport than basketball.
4 Basketball is a .... sport than climbing.
5 Travelling by car is .... than walking.
6 Walking is .... than travelling by car.
7 Winter weather is usually .... in California than in the UK.
8 Winter weather is usually .... in the UK than in California.
9 Learning English is .... for other Europeans than learning Chinese.
10 Learning Chinese is .... for other Europeans than learning English.

good
far
cheap
safe
easy
bad
expensive
near
difficult
dangerous

Grammar: Superlatives

2 Complete the sentences using the correct form of the adjectives.

1 Mount Everest is 8,848 metres. It's the .... mountain in the world.

long   successful   fast   rich
big   old   strong   high

2 Bill Gates is worth $90 billion. He's the .... man in the world.
3 The MGM Hotel and casino in Las Vegas has 5,005 rooms. It's the .... hotel in the world.
4 The St Gothard tunnel in Switzerland is 16.32 kilometres from end to end. It's the .... road tunnel in the world.
5 Brazil is the .... football team in the world. It has won the World Cup four times.
6 Maurice Green ran 100 metres in 9.79 seconds in Greece in 1999. He was the .... man in the world.
7 Sirimavo Bandaranaike became Prime Minister of Sri Lanka at the age of 78 in 1994. She was the .... person in the world to become a PM.
8 Dimitry Kinkladze lifted 48 kilograms with his ears in 1997. He has the .... ears in the world.

Over to you

Use words in the first box to make your own sentences of comparison. Write about yourself, your job, your organisation and your town or city.

Mount Everest is 8,848 metres.

Work vocabulary: How you feel about your job

1 Read about what Miguel thinks about his job.

'Hello. My name's Miguel Hernandez. I work in the accounts department of a food company in Madrid. I quite like my job but not everything is perfect. I get on well with the people I work with and the money is quite good but I live a long way from my office and it takes me almost an hour and a half to get to and from work by car. I also have to work late in the evenings quite often so that sometimes my children are in bed by the time I get home. In fact, I hardly see them at all during the week. I would like to have more time for my family and for myself. My job is not very exciting but I do have the chance to visit one of our factories in another part of Spain once a month and I enjoy that. It's not a very big company and that's good because I prefer working in a smaller organisation.'

Circle the tick for the things Miguel talks about and circle the cross for the things he doesn't mention in items 1–12. Then circle the plus for the things he is positive about and the minus for the things he is negative about.

1 travel to work ✓ ✗ + –
2 travel on business ✓ ✗ + –
3 pay ✓ ✗ + –
4 colleagues ✓ ✗ + –
5 office ✓ ✗ + –
6 hours ✓ ✗ + –

7 holidays ✓ ✗ + –
8 variety ✓ ✗ + –
9 interest ✓ ✗ + –
10 size of the company ✓ ✗ + –
11 work–life balance ✓ ✗ + –
12 company restaurant ✓ ✗ + –

Professional communication: Writing emails

2 An organisation wants its people to be good emailers but the rules are wrong. How can you improve them?

1 Check your emails every week.
2 Save all your old emails.
3 Write long emails. Your colleagues have time to read long emails.
4 Use your office computer for personal emails.
5 Print out all the emails you send and receive.
6 Send copies of all your emails to all your colleagues.

3 Write short (one or two sentence) answers to these emails.

1 Dear David, The meeting has been changed from 4 to 6 on Thursday. Is this OK with you?
2 Hello. My plane gets in at 11 on Tuesday. How do I get to your office?
3 Hi Felicity, I can't open the attachment. Please will you send it again?
4 Dear Sir/Madam, Please send me your latest sales brochure.

 **Over to you**

Write about how you feel about your job. Use the same headings (1–12) as in exercise 1.

Unit 12

General communication: Responses in small talk

1 Match the two halves of each conversation.

1 I've got a new job.
2 What are you doing at the weekend?
3 I went jogging last night.
4 I have to work late tonight.
5 They're going to close the department.
6 Everyone is going to get more money from next week.
7 Tell me if you hear any more news about them.
8 I have a meeting with the boss tomorrow.

a Never mind. We'll go out tomorrow.
b Of course I will.
c I'm not sure yet.
d I can't believe it.
e Oh yes? Why's that?
f That's great news.
g You're joking. You never do that!
h Well done. Congratulations!

General vocabulary: Sport and physical exercise

2 Write the correct verb in each circle: do, play, go and take.

the dog for a walk

the children to the park

chess

bridge

golf

football

camping

for walks in the country

fishing

to the gym

aerobics

yoga

weight training

a lot of sport

3 Complete what these people are saying with words from the box.

outdoor	team	individual	fit	indoor

1 I like to do lots of sport. It keeps me ....
2 I prefer .... activities like walking and camping.
3 I prefer .... activities like chess and bridge.
4 I prefer .... sports like football and basketball.
5 I prefer .... sports like swimming and running.

 **Over to you**

How do you keep fit? Write down: • three activities and sports which you like to do
• three which you like to watch
• three which you don't like.

Grammar: Past simple – your professional background

1 Alfred is talking about his background. Complete these sentences, using one of the verbs in the box. Put each verb into the correct form of the past simple.

1 I .... school at 16.

2 I didn't .... very good qualifications.

3 I .... a job designing computer games.

4 I .... there for three years.

5 I .... to leave because I was bored.

6 I .... to another company but I didn't
.... it very much.

7 So I .... for a diploma in website design.

8 I .... the software for a new game.

9 The game was good and I .... my own company.

> decide
> like
> write
> study
> leave
> start
> get
> stay
> have
> move

Grammar: Past simple – question forms and irregular verbs

2 Complete the conversation with the correct questions or answers.

SYLVIE: Where .... you .... (go) last week?

JOHNNY: I .... (go) to New York.

SYLVIE: Why?

JOHNNY: I .... (have) a meeting with my agent.

SYLVIE: .... the meeting .... (go) well?

JOHNNY: Yes, she .... (tell) me some interesting things.

SYLVIE: When .... you .... (get) back?

JOHNNY: About six on Friday morning.

SYLVIE: What .... you .... (do) on Saturday?

JOHNNY: I .... (go) to the casino
and I .... (win) €10,000.

Over to you

Write down: • three things you did yesterday
• three things you did last weekend
• three things you did last year.

Unit 14

Work vocabulary: Your organisation

1 Match the answers (a–e) with these questions (1–5) about an organisation. You must also add one word to each question to complete it.

1 When was Arco Games .... ?
2 What is the main .... of the company?
3 Where is the company .... ?
4 How is the company .... ?
5 Who sells the .... ?

a You can buy them in most computer game shops.
b It has five main departments.
c It makes computer games.
d In 1981.
e The head office is in Birmingham.

Professional communication: Visiting an organisation

2 Here is a scrambled conversation between a visitor to a company and the receptionist. Number the sentences in the right order. The first one has been done for you.

☐ Do you have a passport or an identity card?

☐ 9 o'clock.

☐ Mr Pierron's secretary will come down to meet you in five minutes. Would you like a coffee?

☐ Yes, here you are.

☐ Thank you. Please will you wear this visitor's badge and take a seat. I'll call his secretary.

☐ No thanks.

☐ Sure.

1 Good morning, I have a meeting with Mr Pierron.

☐ Good morning. What time is your appointment?

☐ OK. Just let me know if there's anything you need.

3 You have a visitor. Think of a word to complete each sentence.

1 Can I get you something to .... ? We have coffee, tea and fruit juice.

2 Would you mind starting at ten past nine? I'm afraid Mrs Sanchez will be a few minutes ....

3 Did you arrive this morning? Did you have a good .... ?

4 It rained here all last week. How is the .... in London?

5 Where are you .... ? How is your hotel?

Over to you

Write down 1 the names in English of three jobs and three departments in your organisation; 2 three things you can say to visitors to your organisation.

General communication: Getting there

1 Complete the sentences with words from the box.

1 Can I .... in here?

2 Please may I see your .... ?

gate	aisle	passport
check	delay	

3 Would you like a window seat or an .... seat, madam?

4 Boarding is at .... 27 in half an hour.

5 We are very sorry for the ....

2 Put the verbs in the order in which they happen.

Airport:	land	take off	board	check in
Taxi:	get in	tip	book	get out of
Train:	change	depart	arrive	go to the station
Coach:	buy a ticket	sleep	get off	get on

3 Match the first half of each travel phrase with the second half on the right.

1 business	desk
2 window	locker
3 boarding	reservation
4 flight	luggage
5 seat	class
6 overhead	seat
7 check-in	information
8 hand	pass

General vocabulary: Holidays and travel

4 Match the verbs (1–10) with the holiday activities (a–j).

1 play	a mountains
2 sunbathe	b cars
3 climb	c sightseeing
4 visit	d on beaches
5 go on	e hotels
6 ski	f tennis
7 see	g coach tours
8 stay in	h off-piste
9 hire	i museums
10 go	j shows at the theatre

 **Over to you**

Write down five things you like doing on holiday and five things you don't like doing.

Unit 16

Grammar: Present continuous

1 What is Edith doing at the moment? Complete each sentence with the present continuous form of the verb.

1 It's 7.30. Edith is eating a croissant. She .... breakfast. (have)

2 It's 8.30. She's in her car. She .... to work. (drive)

3 It's 9.00. She's on her computer. She .... her emails. (check)

4 It's 10.00. She's on the phone. She .... her biggest customer. (call)

5 It's 11.00. She's with her colleagues. She .... the departmental meeting. (attend)

6 It's 4.30. She's talking to the senior management committee.
   She .... an important presentation. (make)

Grammar: Present continuous and present simple – asking questions

2 Which is the correct tense to use in this conversation? Cross out the questions which are wrong.

1 Q: What do you do? / What are you doing?
   A: I'm a marketing consultant.

2 Q: Who do you work for? / Who are you working for?
   A: I work for myself. I'm self-employed.

3 Q: Who are you working with at the moment? / Who do you work with at the moment?
   A: I'm working with a small company in London.

4 Q: What does it do? / What is it doing?
   A: It makes software.

5 Q: And why are you working for them? / Why do you work for them?
   A: Because they are trying to increase their sales in the USA.

6 Q: Where do you live? / Where are you living?
   A: I live in Edinburgh.

7 Q: Are you working on any other projects at the moment? / Do you work on any other projects at the moment?
   A: Yes, I'm working on a new marketing campaign for a travel agency in Glasgow.

8 Q: Do you go to Glasgow a lot? / Are you going to Glasgow a lot?
   A: Yes, I go there three or four times a month.

 **Over to you**

What are you working on at the moment? Write complete sentences about three of your current projects.

Work vocabulary: Communicating at work

1 Look at the communication verbs in these sentences and find the mistake in each one. What is the correct sentence?

1 We discussed about the sales figures for nearly an hour.
2 We talked to the sales figures for nearly an hour.
3 The marketing director said him lots of nice things.
4 The marketing director told to him to work harder.
5 I asked to the secretary about the time of the meeting.
6 He tried to explain it me but I couldn't understand it.
7 She presented us the latest sales figures yesterday.
8 I will call to you about this tomorrow.
9 I will phone to you about this tomorrow.
10 I listened him for half an hour but it wasn't very interesting.

Professional communication: Writing emails

2 The phrases in the box are from a formal business letter and a more informal email. Match them up and write them in the table.

	Formal letter	Informal email
Greeting		
Beginning		
Information / action point		
Close		

With reference to your enquiry, ...   Hi Sara   Regards   Thanks for your email
I look forward to hearing from you soon   Please send me your doc.   Dear Mrs Smith
I should be grateful if you would send me a copy of your brochure

 **Over to you**

Who did you communicate with last week? Write sentences starting:
I called ...   I discussed ...   I talked ...   I told ...   I asked ...

Unit 18

General communication: In the restaurant

1 **Number the sentences 1–10 to put them in the right order.**

I'll have the duck, please.

Could we have some more bread, please?

Can I have the bill, please?

Thank you. It was excellent.

What do you recommend?

Thank you. Enjoy the rest of your stay.

Are you ready to order, madam?

Good evening, sir.

Would you like an aperitif?

Good evening. Can we have a table for four, please?

General vocabulary: Food and drink

2 **Complete the following sentences.**

1 Are you ready to order? No! We have to look at the m................................ first!

2 Do you want a starter? No thanks, I think I'll go straight to the m................................ c................................ .

3 We'd like to order some wine. Can we see the w................................ l................................ , please?

4 We'd also like some water, please: one bottle of s................................ and one of s................................ , please.

5 The main course is served with a selection of v................................ – potatoes, carrots and courgettes.

6 I'm sorry, I don't eat meat or fish. I'm a v................................ .

7 I'll have chicken and a green s................................ , please.

8 Would you like to finish with c................................ or a d................................ ?

Could we have some more bread, please?

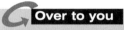**Over to you**

What is your favourite national cuisine? Which are your favourite foods? What is your favourite three course meal?

Grammar: *Should* and *have to*

1 Rewrite each of the sentences using You should, You shouldn't,
You have to or You don't have to.

1 It's necessary for you to be at work by 8.30.

2 It's not necessary for you to have lunch in the canteen.

3 I think it's a bad idea to use so much paper.

4 It's necessary for you to wear a suit and tie when
you meet clients.

5 I think it's a good idea for you to meet the new
Human Resources director.

6 It's necessary for you to leave before 6 if you
want to catch your plane.

7 I think it's a bad idea for you to go to Paris next week.

8 I think it's a good idea for you to leave work early during
the school holidays.

9 Finish the report. It's the rule!

10 It's not necessary for you to get up early on Saturday.

2 Change these sentences into <u>questions</u> using should or have to.

1 It's necessary for him to change planes in Singapore.

2 It's a good idea for them to be out so late.

3 It's necessary for them to bring all the papers.

4 It's a good idea for us to talk to them more.

5 It's necessary for them to work harder.

Pronunciation: Word stress

3 How many syllables are there in these words? Which is the stressed
syllable?

	Number of syllables	Stressed syllable (1st, 2nd, ...)
syllable		
organisation		
fantastic		
vegetable		
photographer		

 **Over to you**

Write down sentences to say three things you have to do in your job and three things
you don't have to do in your job.

Unit 20

Work vocabulary: Computers and the Internet

1 **Number the phrases in the right order 1–8.**

send your replies ▢ switch off ▢ open your emails ▢ connect to the Internet ▢
disconnect from the Internet ▢ log on ▢ switch on your computer ▢ enter your password ▢

2 **Match the verbs with the definitions.**

1	Point and click	a	You do this when you transfer something from a disk or another computer to your PC.
2	Pull down	b	You do this when you make a second version of something.
3	Save	c	You do this when you send a file to the Recycle Bin.
4	Crash	d	You do this with a menu to read the list.
5	Surf	e	You do this with the mouse.
6	Download	f	You do this so that you do not lose your work.
7	Delete	g	When your computer stops working.
8	Copy	h	You do this when you visit different sites on the Internet.

Professional communication: Arranging meetings by phone

3 **Match the pairs of phrases which mean the same.**

have a meeting	put back a meeting
cancel a meeting	be at a meeting
postpone a meeting	hold a meeting
fix a meeting	arrange a meeting
take part in a meeting	not have a meeting

4 **Match the sentences with the stages in the phone call.**

Open the call	How about next Thursday, the 17th?
Ask for a meeting	11 o'clock no good? How about 12? OK? Fine.
The reason	Can you send me these details by email, please?
The date	Hello Regina, it's Guy. How are you?
The time	I can come to your office if you like.
Agree	Guy, can we have a meeting soon?
The place	11 o'clock would be good for me.
Ask for confirmation	We need to discuss the new computer network.

> **⌕ Over to you**
>
> Write your own sentences for each of the stages in organising a meeting on the phone: Open the call → Ask for a meeting, etc.

General communication: Staying at hotels

1 The underlined words are wrong. Change them to make sentences that people say in hotels.

1 I'd like one <u>single</u> room for my wife and myself, please.
2 Please could you be <u>in</u> your room by 10.30 on the morning you check out.
3 You can ask for your bill in <u>the lift</u> when you leave.
4 Would you like an aperitif <u>after</u> your meal, madam?
5 And what would you like to <u>eat</u> with your meal, sir?
6 I'll have the soup as a <u>main course</u> and then chicken, please.
7 How much is a room? Does that <u>exclude</u> everything?
8 Would you order a <u>train</u> for me, please?

General vocabulary: Hotels

2 Where do you do these things in a hotel?

1 Have a drink	in your bedroom
2 Eat a meal	in the gym
3 Pay your bill	in the lift (British English) / elevator (American English)
4 Park your car	through an emergency exit
5 Order a meal for your room	in the lounge
6 Take some exercise	in the bar
7 Leave if there's a fire	in the dining room
8 Go up to your room	in the garage
9 Sit and read your newspaper	in reception
10 Sleep	from room service

3 The jobs of these hotel people have got mixed up. Can you match them up correctly?

1 The wine waiter	makes your bed and cleans your room
2 The guest	looks after the staff
3 The porter	carries your bag to your room
4 The receptionist	opens the door of your taxi
5 The waiter	serves your meals
6 The manager	pays to stay in the hotel
7 The chambermaid	brings you your drinks in the restaurant
8 The doorman	checks you in when you arrive

Over to you

1 Write down five things which are important in a good hotel.
2 What is the best hotel you have ever stayed in? Why?

Unit 22

Grammar: *Many* and *much*

1 Choose many or much in each of these sentences.

1 How *many* / *much* people work at the hospital?
2 How *many* / *much* staff does the hospital employ?
3 How *many* / *much* time did it take?
4 How *many* / *much* hours did it take?
5 How *many* / *much* holiday do you plan to take this year?
6 How *many* / *much* weeks' holiday do you plan to take this year?
7 How *many* / *much* furniture is there in your office?
8 How *many* / *much* desks are there in your office?

Grammar: *A few* and *a little*

2 Choose a few or a little in each of these sentences.

1 His company only has *a few* / *a little* employees.
2 I only have *a few* / *a little* time left.
3 I can only give you *a few* / *a little* news about the situation.
4 He usually drinks just *a few* / *a little* wine because it makes him feel ill.
5 We think that there will be *a few* / *a little* rain this evening.
6 I'm sure she'll arrive in just *a few* / *a little* minutes.
7 It will cost *a few* / *a little* money to repair all the equipment.
8 I want to give you *a few* / *a little* words of advice.

3 Quiz Can you answer these general knowledge questions?

1 How many countries are members of the United Nations?
   a) 157   b) 184   c) 191   d) 203
2 How much information is produced per year for every man, woman and child on earth?
   a) 10 megabytes   b) 50 megabytes   c) 150 megabytes   d) 250 megabytes
3 How many people live in Japan (2002 figure)?
   a) 103 million   b) 127 million   c) 145 million   d) 161 million
4 How many different Nobel prizes are there?
   a) 5   b) 6   c) 7   d) 8
5 How much wine does the average French person drink every year?
   a) 8 litres   b) 27 litres   c) 40 litres   d) 53 litres

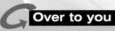 **Over to you**

You meet someone from a country you do not know very much about. Write down four or five questions beginning *How much . . . ?* and *How many . . . ?* to get more information about the country.

Work vocabulary: Money and finance

1 Match one word from the box with each sentence about the finances of a small company.

> paying   invoicing   investing   saving   borrowing   planning

1 We decide the budget at the beginning of every year.   ....
2 We asked the bank for a loan to open a new office.   ....
3 We cut the size of our electricity and telecoms bills.   ....
4 We write cheques for our suppliers very quickly.   ....
5 We send a bill to customers when we send their order.   ....
6 We spent a lot of money on a new factory.   ....

2 Finish each second sentence with a word from the box which means the opposite of the underlined word in the first.

> increase   sell   save   lend

1 We <u>buy</u> British pounds at a rate of one euro 47 cents per pound.
   We .... pounds at a rate of 65 pence per euro.
2 We want to <u>borrow</u> another million dollars from the bank. The bank
   says it will not .... us another million dollars.
3 Every year we <u>reduce</u> our costs. Every year we .... our prices.
4 At the moment I <u>spend</u> 95% of my income. I have decided
   to .... 10% of my income this year.

Professional communication: Helping visitors

3 Match the visitor's problems with the responses.

1 Your visitor can't find her passport.
2 Her suitcase got lost in transit.
3 She has another appointment in one
   hour at another company.
4 She doesn't know how to get to her
   next appointment.
5 She is late and the person she wants
   to meet is in another meeting.

I'll tell Mr Smith that you'd
like to leave in half an hour.
I'll book you a taxi.
Where did you last see it?
I'm afraid Mr Jones is in a
meeting now. I'll tell him
you're here.
I'll call the airline.

 **Over to you**

Money is important in everyone's working life. Write four sentences to say how it is important in your job.

Unit 24

General communication: Money for shopping and travel

1 **Put the words in the right order in each sentence.**

1 I money can where some change?
2 charge do commission you?
3 nearest tell is point the me can cash you where?
4 of rate what the exchange is?
5 credit accept you cards do?
6 give receipt a can you me?
7 two you can hundred euro change a note?

General vocabulary: Money

2 **Match the words and pictures.**

cash machine   cheque   coins   bank card   cheque book   notes

1 ....   2 ....   3 ....   4 ....   5 ....   6 ....

3 Managing your money   **Choose one verb from the box for each sentence. Make sure you use the correct form of the verb.**

| send   tell   take   pay   get   earn   open   use   save   write |

1 I think you should .... a bank account.
2 Your employer can .... the money into your account at the end of every month.
3 You can .... money from the account when you want.
4 Every month the bank .... you a bank statement.
5 This .... you how much money there is in the account.
6 If you want to .... money, you can have a savings account.
7 The money in your savings account can .... interest of 2 or 3 per cent, depending on the current rates.
8 When you want to pay for things, you can .... a cheque.
9 Or you can .... your bank card.
10 You can also use your bank card to .... money from a cash machine when the banks are closed.

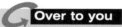
Over to you

What rate of interest does your bank pay? How often do you get a statement?
Write four sentences about you, your bank and your bank account.

Grammar: Present continuous for future plans

1 Rosemary Canter has a busy life at the top. Complete the sentences with the correct form of the verbs in the box.

open	have	stay	play	go	attend	meet

1 Ms Canter .... to a senior management meeting next week.

2 Next month she .... a government minister in London.

3 Tomorrow she .... a big conference in Paris.

4 At the weekend she .... at home in London.

5 On Sunday evening she .... an art exhibition in Edinburgh.

6 This afternoon she .... golf with her husband.

7 In the summer she .... a three week holiday in the Maldives.

2 Two people are talking at a trade fair. Complete their conversation with the correct form of the verbs in the box.

A: Hi! Enjoying it?

B: Not really. Pretty boring in fact. Let's do something else.

A: Good idea. When?

B: Now?

A: I can't. I (1) .... my boss in ten minutes. How about this afternoon?

B: I can't. I (2) .... to our product launch.

A: What about after that?

B: No, sorry. I (3) .... a colleague for a drink at the end of the afternoon.

A: OK, what about tomorrow morning?

B: That's difficult too. The people from South America (4) .... at 10 o'clock. But I could be free after 12.

A: Sorry, I (5) .... a working lunch with my team.

B: Never mind. I (6) .... anything tomorrow afternoon.

A: Nor me. Let's go out then.

B: Great. Maybe I can get some tickets for the tennis.

A: Wonderful. See you here at 2.30?

B: It's a deal!

go
have
see
not / do
meet
arrive

A holiday in the Maldives

Over to you

Write some sentences describing your plans for:

• tonight   • the weekend   • next week   • next month   • in the summer

Unit 26

Work vocabulary: Solving problems

1 Choose one verb from the box to complete each sentence.

1 We .... a major technical problem with the computer network.

2 We have to .... a solution quickly.

3 I'm sure our technical staff can .... the problem.

4 If the problem continues, our customers will ....

> complain
> solve
> have
> find

2 Problems at work Match what people say with the problems in the box.

> quality   organisation   slow payers   stress   time   understaffing
> a difficult colleague   work environment   customer service

1 I tried to talk to him but he doesn't want to listen.

2 Yesterday we worked until 8 and tonight we have to work late again.

3 I don't know who my boss is and I don't know who's in my team.

4 There's more work but there are only three people in the office – a year ago there were five.

5 Lots of customers say they have problems with our equipment.

6 The office is so noisy and the light is so bad that I often have a headache at the end of the day.

7 I called him again and he said that the cheque is in the post but I know it isn't and he knows that I know.

8 There is too much work, the breaks are not long enough, my boss is always angry and I always feel tired.

9 When clients call, there is often nobody to answer the phone.

Professional communication: Solving problems by phone

3 Here are some expressions which problem solvers use on the phone. Complete each sentence with a word from the box.

1 How can I .... you?

2 What .... is the problem?

3 There must be an .... to this problem.

4 We can .... a solution to this.

5 I'll .... what I can do.

6 Why don't you .... switching it off and on again?

> answer
> see
> try
> help
> exactly
> find

Over to you

Write four sentences about you and your computer. What do you use it for? How much do you use it? What problems do you have with it?

General communication: Making invitations

1 Complete each sentence with a word from the box and then choose the more polite answer for each of these invitations.

1 Would you .... to come to dinner on Saturday night?
a) Thanks. I'd love to.   b) What time will it finish?

2 .... you come to the cinema next week?
a) That'd be nice. What's on?   b) Will you pay?

3 Are you .... on Friday evening? We're having a party.
a) I don't know.   b) Thanks, but I'm not sure. Can I let you know tomorrow?

4 How .... a game of tennis at the weekend?
a) I can't. I'm busy.   b) I'd like to but I'm afraid I'm busy all weekend.

like
can
about
free

General vocabulary: Health and fitness

2 Complete these sentences about health and fitness.

1 Smoking is bad for your .... and lungs. H ▨ ▨ ▨ ▨

2 You should try to take some physical .... every day. E ▨ ▨ ▨ ▨ ▨ ▨

3 If you eat too many biscuits and chocolates, you will get .... ▨ A ▨

4 Most people need seven or eight hours' .... every night. ▨ L ▨ ▨

5 I must go on a .... because I am overweight. ▨ ▨ ▨ T

6 To eat well you should eat lots of .... fruit and vegetables. ▨ ▨ ▨ ▨ H

7 Some people drive their cars just a few hundred metres because they are too .... to walk or cycle. ▨ ▨ ▨ Y

8 I must cut down on eating and drinking because I need to .... weight. L ▨ ▨ ▨

9 I want to be as .... as I was when I bought this swimming costume. ▨ ▨ I ▨

10 This year I really want to .... up smoking. ▨ ▨ V ▨

11 People who smoke and drink a lot often don't .... as long as they could. ▨ I ▨ ▨

12 I'm going to stop eating .... foods like hamburgers and chips. ▨ N ▨ ▨ ▨ ▨ ▨ ▨

13 Since I stopped eating chocolate, my .... has gone down by several kilos. ▨ ▨ ▨ G ▨ ▨

HEALTHY LIVING

Over to you What would you say to invite someone:
• to go to the cinema • to have dinner at your house • to go to a restaurant for dinner
• to play golf • to stay in your country house for the weekend?

Unit 28

Grammar: Present perfect

1 Read what Victor says about his life and what other people say about him. Put the verbs into the present perfect.

1 I .... to almost every country in the world. (be)

2 I .... hundreds of companies in the US and Europe. (buy)

3 I .... how to fly a jumbo jet. (learn)

4 I .... the Presidents of both the USA and China. (meet)

5 He .... never .... to the US President. (speak)

6 He .... never .... in the pilot's seat of a jumbo jet. (sit)

7 He .... never .... Japan, China or Russia. (visit)

8 He .... never .... a company. (own)

2 Birgit is with Sophie talking to a customer at a trade fair. Complete her questions with the correct form of the verb. Then complete the replies and choose the best one for each sentence.

1 meet	Have you .... Sophie?	Replies
2 see	Have you .... our brochure?	No. Not .... ! No, not yet. .... you?
3 buy	Have you ever .... any of our products?	No, I .... Nice to meet you.
4 be	Have you ever .... to the USA?	Yes, I .... It's very good.
5 have	Have you .... lunch yet?	Yes. I've .... there twice.

3 Katherine and her boss, Nicola, meet after an exhibition. Complete the discussion with the correct form of the verb in the present perfect.

KATHERINE: Great news! We (receive) (1) .... three big new orders since the exhibition. Elena Products (order) (2) .... 50,000 of our new skin lotion.

NICOLA: That's excellent.

KATHERINE: Perfect Hair and Serena Cosmetics (also / agree) (3) .... to buy 20,000 of our special shampoo.

NICOLA: Great. Are they new customers? (they / ever / buy) (4) .... our products before?

KATHERINE: No. They're both new customers. (We / never / sell) (5) .... any of our products to these two companies.

NICOLA: Great! You've done really well.

Over to you

Write down five things that you are proud to have done in your life so far.

Work vocabulary: Trends

1 Look at this graph showing sales of a magazine. Then complete the sentences with words from the box. Use the correct form of the verbs.

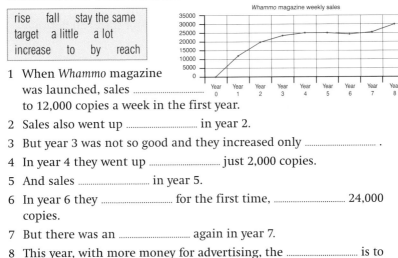

Whammo magazine weekly sales

rise	fall	stay the same
target	a little	a lot
increase	to	by	reach

1 When *Whammo* magazine was launched, sales .... to 12,000 copies a week in the first year.

2 Sales also went up .... in year 2.

3 But year 3 was not so good and they increased only ....

4 In year 4 they went up .... just 2,000 copies.

5 And sales .... in year 5.

6 In year 6 they .... for the first time, ... 24,000 copies.

7 But there was an .... again in year 7.

8 This year, with more money for advertising, the .... is to .... sales of 30,000 copies a week for the first time.

Professional communication: Arranging meetings by email

2 Complete each sentence with a word from the box.

| meet | free | convenient | fix | holiday | let's | forward | busy | make | agenda |

RUTH: Could we (1) .... a meeting for next Monday?

PAUL: I'm sorry. I'm on (2) .... all next week.

RUTH: OK. In that case, are you (3) .... on Friday?

PAUL: Yes. Friday's OK. Is the morning (4) .... for you?

RUTH: I'm sorry, I'm (5) .... all morning. Could we (6) .... it sometime in the afternoon?

PAUL: Listen, (7) .... have lunch and (8) .... at 2.

RUTH: That sounds good. I'll look (9)............................... to it.

PAUL: Great. Can you send me an (10)............................... ?

RUTH: You'll have it by the end of the afternoon.

Over to you

Write sentences about figures for your organisation, e.g. two things which have gone up this year and two things which have gone down.

Unit 30

General vocabulary: Lifestyles

1 Find pairs of sentences about Maria which have the same meaning.

1 She doesn't eat meat.
2 She is a very relaxed person.
3 She doesn't eat fast food.
4 She doesn't get tense.
5 She is semi-retired.
6 She sleeps very well.
7 She has a good work–life balance.

a She gets a good night's rest every night.
b She doesn't spend all her time working.
c She doesn't get stressed.
d She is near the end of her working life but still works part-time.
e She's a vegetarian.
f She doesn't eat junk food.
g She's very laid back.

General vocabulary: Learning vocabulary

2 Build your vocabulary by making word families. Complete the table.

Verb	Person noun	General noun
organise		
	manager	
produce		
compete		
	decision-maker	
		investment

General communication: Saying goodbye

3 Substitute the words in *italics* in each sentence with one of the phrases in the box.

1 See you again *later in the year*.
2 Give my *regards* to Jim.
3 We're looking forward to *the next time*.
4 Until *the next time*.
5 Drive *carefully*.
6 Say hello to Cynthia *for me*.
7 Thanks for *looking after us so well*.
8 It was *really kind* of you to invite us.
9 Have a safe *trip*.
10 *Call* us when you get back.

best wishes
ring
so good
your hospitality
in the autumn
we meet again
from me
journey
safely
the next meeting

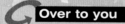 **Over to you**

Write four sentences about yourself and your lifestyle.

Answer key to Practice exercises

Unit 1

Introductions: Meeting people 1
1 1 d   2 h   3 j   4 g   5 i   6 c   7 a   8 f   9 b   10 e

Grammar: Present simple – Meeting people 2
2 1 am   2 Do   3 in   4 work   5 work   6 do   7 am   8 do
      9 do   10 work   11 Do   12 like   13 like   14 don't   15 like

Unit 2

Work vocabulary: Job responsibilities
1 1 d   2 c   3 a   4 b
2 1 I work for a company called PassGo.
      2 I work in the sales department.
      3 I work with people from all over the world.
      4 I work in London.

Professional communication: Telephoning phrases
3 1 Good morning. CDA.
      2 Hello. Could I speak to Sandra Wagner, please?
      3 One moment, please.
      4 Hello. Sandra Wagner.
      5 Good morning, Ms Wagner, this is Joe Stoppard. We met last week.
      6 Oh hello, Mr Stoppard. Yes, I remember. How are you?
      7 Fine thanks, and you?
      8 I'm fine. What can I do for you?
      9 I'd like your brochure. Can you send me one?
      10 Sure. I have your address. I'll send it today.
      11 Thanks a lot. Goodbye.
      12 Goodbye.

Unit 3

General communication: Social talk at the office
1 1 Hello, how are you?
      2 Ready for some lunch?
      3 Where do you want to eat?
      4 Thank goodness it's Friday.
      5 Do you have any plans for the weekend?
      6 I'm going to visit my brother.
      7 See you next week.
      8 Have a good weekend.

General vocabulary: Free-time activities

2 *Pictures in this order:* swimming, playing the guitar, skiing, inviting friends to dinner, theatre, going on holiday with friends, cleaning, ironing, cinema, playing the piano

3 Music: playing the guitar, playing the piano
Sports: swimming, skiing
Culture: cinema, theatre
Socialising: going on holiday with friends, inviting friends to dinner
Housework: ironing, cleaning

Unit 4

Grammar: Present simple – work routines

1   She:

6.30	gets up
7.00	has / makes breakfast
7.30	leaves home
8.00	starts work
8.10	has / makes a cup of coffee
9.00	checks her emails
9.30	works on her computer
11.00	has a meeting with a client
12.00	has lunch
13.30	makes some telephone calls
17.00	finishes work
17.30	gets home
19.00	has / makes dinner
20.00	watches TV
23.30	goes to bed

Grammar: Frequency expressions

2 1 He takes his children to school every day.
2 He often gets phone calls from his main customer in the evenings.
3 He always reads his favourite magazine on Fridays.
4 He usually plays tennis at the weekend.
5 He has a meeting with his boss every two weeks.
6 He visits the main factory in Birmingham once a month.
7 He occasionally has lunch in the company restaurant.
8 He sometimes goes to Spain in the summer.
9 He doesn't go to the Far East very often.
10 He rarely reads a book.
11 He never goes to meetings before 8.30 in the morning.

Unit 5

Work vocabulary: Organisations

1 *Correct sentences:*
1 Who do you work for?
2 What is the main activity of your company?
3 Where is the headquarters of the company?
4 What is the turnover of your company?
5 How many people work for your company?

2 1 Daniel is a consultant. He has a small consultancy in Berlin.
Companies consult him on financial and management questions.
2 I am a personnel manager. I'm very interested in people management.
I manage a team of ten people.
3 Our business is very competitive. We have to compete with a lot of
other companies. Our main competitors are in the USA and Japan.
4 We employ about 3,000 people. About 60% of the employees are
women. We are the biggest employer in the town.

Professional communication: Taking phone messages

3 1 Can I take a message?
2 He's not in the office today.
3 She's away until next Monday.
4 I'll make sure she gets it.
5 Could you ask him to call me back?
6 Could you repeat that?
7 Please will you call back later?
8 Can I have your number?

4 1 N 2 I 3 R 4 Y 5 O 6 V

Unit 6

General communication: Shopping

1 1 Where can I buy a film for my camera?
2 What time does the shop open?
3 Where is the nearest supermarket, please?
4 Do you sell women's shoes?
5 How much is this, please?
6 Can I try it on?
7 Do you have one in a larger size?
8 This is fine. I'll take it.
9 Can I pay by credit card?
10 Can I have a receipt, please?

General vocabulary: Where you live

2 1 Lorenza Tims lives in York.

2 York is a historic city in the north of England.

3 It is about 40 kilometres from the sea.

4 The nearest town on the coast is Scarborough.

5 Scarborough is not far from York.

6 She lives near the city centre, 20 minutes' walk from the cathedral.

7 Her house is in a quiet street near the main road to Leeds.

8 York is about 30 kilometres north-east of Leeds.

3 A: How do you get / travel to work?

B: I take the bus.

A: Where do you catch it?

B: I walk to the supermarket. A bus goes / leaves from there every ten minutes.

Unit 7

Grammar: *There is* and *there are*; *some* and *any*; countable and uncountable nouns

1 1 There are two training rooms on the first floor.

2 There's a reception area on the ground floor.

3 There are some open plan offices on the second floor.

4 There's a lot of computer equipment on the first floor.

5 There are a lot of offices on the top floor.

6 There's a large car park next to the building.

7 There's the latest company news on the computer in reception.

8 There's no swimming pool.

2 1 Did you hear the news about the president?

2 Did you get any information about prices?

3 I gave him some money but he said it wasn't enough.

4 I think we need some time to solve this problem.

5 He lost a suitcase at the airport.

6 He lost some luggage at the airport.

7 We have a problem with the computer again.

8 He has a good job but at the moment he doesn't have any work to do.

Unit 8

Work vocabulary: Describing people

1 1 d 2 g 3 i 4 f 5 a 6 h 7 j 8 c 9 b 10 e

2 inefficient   unpopular   disorganised   indirect   impatient   untidy   unreliable   insensitive   dishonest   inexperienced

Professional communication: Meeting a visitor at the airport

3 MAY: Excuse me. Are you Mr Ducroix from Lambert Holdings?

PIERRE: Yes, that's right. Pierre Ducroix. And are you May Lester?

MAY: Yes. Pleased to meet you.

PIERRE: Nice to meet you. Thanks for coming to meet me.

MAY: Not at all. It's only 20 minutes from the office. Welcome to Edinburgh. How was the trip?

PIERRE: It was good. I had a sleep and did some work, and the food was OK.

MAY: And how's the weather in Paris?

PIERRE: It's awful. It doesn't stop raining!

MAY: Oh dear. Well, it's good here. Can I help you with your bags?

PIERRE: No thanks, I'm OK.

MAY: Good. Well, the car's in the car park just over there . . .

Unit 9

General communication: Getting around

1 a cab – a taxi; a bus – a coach; the subway – the underground; a boat – a ferry

2 1 g   2 a   3 h   4 c   5 e   6 b   7 d   8 f

General vocabulary: Where you live

3 1 j   2 f   3 g   4 h   5 a   6 i   7 e   8 d   9 c   10 b

Unit 10

Grammar: Comparatives

1 1 Tokyo is nearer to Beijing than Washington.

2 Washington is further from Tokyo than Beijing.

3 Climbing is a more dangerous sport than basketball.

4 Basketball is a safer sport than climbing.

5 Travelling by car is more expensive than walking.

6 Walking is cheaper than travelling by car.

7 Winter weather is usually better in California than in the UK.

8 Winter weather is usually worse in the UK than in California.

9 Learning English is easier for other Europeans than learning Chinese.

10 Learning Chinese is more difficult for other Europeans than learning English.

Grammar: Superlatives

2 1 Mount Everest is 8,848 metres. It's the highest mountain in the world.

2 Bill Gates is worth $90 billion. He's the richest man in the world.

3 The MGM Hotel and casino in Las Vegas has 5,005 rooms. It's the biggest hotel in the world.

4 The St Gothard tunnel in Switzerland is 16.32 kilometres from end to end. It's the longest road tunnel in the world.

5 Brazil is the most successful football team in the world. It has won the World Cup four times.

6 Maurice Green ran 100 metres in 9.79 seconds in Greece in 1999. He was the fastest man in the world.

7 Sirimavo Bandaranaike became Prime Minister of Sri Lanka at the age of 78 in 1994. She was the oldest person in the world to become a PM.

8 Dimitry Kinkladze lifted 48 kilograms with his ears in 1997. He has the strongest ears in the world.

Unit 11

Work vocabulary: How you feel about your job

1
1	travel to work	✓	−
2	travel on business	✓	+
3	pay	✓	+
4	colleagues	✓	+
5	office	✗	
6	hours	✓	−
7	holidays	✗	
8	variety	✗	
9	interest	✓	−
10	size of the company	✓	+
11	work–life balance	✓	−
12	company restaurant	✗	

Professional communication: Writing emails

2 1 Check your emails every day / two or three times a day.

2 Don't save / Delete all your old emails.

3 Write short emails. Your colleagues don't have time to read long emails.

4 Don't use your office computer for personal emails.

5 Don't print out all the emails you send and receive.

6 Don't send copies of all your emails to all your colleagues.

3 *Possible answers:*

1 It's fine with me.
2 Take a taxi.
3 Sorry. Here it is again.
4 Thank you for your email. We are sending you our brochure today.

Unit 12

General communication: Responses in small talk
1 1 h   2 c   3 g   4 a   5 d   6 f   7 b   8 e

General vocabulary: Sport and physical exercise
2 Do: aerobics, weight training, yoga, a lot of sport
Play: chess, bridge, golf, football
Go: to the gym, camping, for walks in the country, fishing
Take: the dog for a walk, the children to the park

3 1 I like to do lots of sports. It keeps me fit.
2 I prefer outdoor activities like walking and camping.
3 I prefer indoor activities like chess and bridge.
4 I prefer team sports like football and basketball.
5 I prefer individual sports like swimming and running.

Unit 13

Grammar: Past simple – your professional background
1 1 I left school at 16.
2 I didn't have / get very good qualifications.
3 I got a job designing computer games.
4 I stayed there for three years.
5 I decided to leave because I was bored.
6 I moved to another company but I didn't like it very much.
7 So I studied for a diploma in website design.
8 I wrote the software for a new game.
9 The game was good and I started my own company

Grammar: Past simple – question forms and irregular verbs
2 SYLVIE: Where did you go last week?
JOHNNY: I went to New York.
SYLVIE: Why?
JOHNNY: I had a meeting with my agent.
SYLVIE: Did the meeting go well?
JOHNNY: Yes, she told me some interesting things.
SYLVIE: When did you get back?
JOHNNY: About six on Friday morning.
SYLVIE: What did you do on Saturday?
JOHNNY: I went to the casino and I won €10,000.

Unit 14

Work vocabulary: Your organisation

1 1 d When was Arco Games started?
2 c What is the main activity of the company?
3 e Where is the company located / based?
4 b How is the company organised?
5 a Who sells the products?

Professional communication: Visiting an organisation

2 1 Good morning, I have a meeting with Mr Pierron.
2 Good morning. What time is your appointment?
3 9 o'clock.
4 Do you have a passport or an identity card?
5 Yes, here you are.
6 Thank you. Please will you wear this visitor's badge and take a seat. I'll call his secretary.
7 Sure.
8 Mr Pierron's secretary will come down to meet you in five minutes. Would you like a coffee?
9 No thanks.
10 OK. Just let me know if there's anything you need.

3 1 Can I get you something to drink? We have coffee, tea and fruit juice.
2 Would you mind starting at ten past nine? I'm afraid Mrs Sanchez will be a few minutes late.
3 Did you arrive this morning? Did you have a good trip / journey / flight?
4 It rained here all last week. How is the weather in London?
5 Where are you staying? How is your hotel?

Unit 15

General communication: Getting there

1 1 Can I check in here?
2 Please may I see your passport?
3 Would you like a window seat or an aisle seat, madam?
4 Boarding is at gate 27 in half an hour.
5 We are very sorry for the delay.

2 Airport: check in – board – take off – land
Taxi: book – get in – tip – get out of
Train: go to the station – depart – change – arrive
Coach: buy a ticket – get on – sleep – get off

3 1 business class
2 window seat
3 boarding pass
4 flight information
5 seat reservation
6 overhead locker
7 check-in desk
8 hand luggage

General vocabulary: Holidays and travel
4 1 f 2 d 3 a 4 i 5 g 6 h 7 j 8 e 9 b 10 c

Unit 16

Grammar: Present continuous
1 1 She is having breakfast.
2 She is driving to work.
3 She is checking her emails.
4 She is calling her biggest customer.
5 She is attending the departmental meeting.
6 She is making an important presentation.

Grammar: Present continuous and present simple – asking questions
2 1 What do you do?
2 Who do you work for?
3 Who are you working with at the moment?
4 What does it do?
5 And why are you working for them?
6 Where do you live?
7 Are you working on any other projects at the moment?
8 Do you go to Glasgow a lot?

Unit 17

Work vocabulary: Communicating at work
1 1 We discussed the sales figures for nearly an hour.
2 We talked about the sales figures for nearly an hour.
3 The marketing director said lots of nice things to him / told him lots of nice things.
4 The marketing director told him to work harder.
5 I asked the secretary about the time of the meeting.
6 He tried to explain it to me but I couldn't understand it.
7 She presented the latest sales figures to us yesterday / She presented us with …

8 I will call you about this tomorrow.
9 I will phone you about this tomorrow.
10 I listened to him for half an hour but it wasn't very interesting.

Professional communication: Writing emails
2

	Formal letter	Informal email
Greeting	Dear Mrs Smith	Hi Sara
Beginning	With reference to your enquiry, ...	Thanks for your email
Information / action point	I should be grateful if you would send me a copy of your brochure	Please send me your doc.
Close	I look forward to hearing from you soon	Regards

Unit 18

General communication: In the restaurant
1 1 Good evening, sir.
   2 Good evening. Can we have a table for four, please?
   3 Would you like an aperitif?
   4 Are you ready to order, madam?
   5 What do you recommend?
   6 I'll have the duck, please.
   7 Could we have some more bread, please?
   8 Can I have the bill, please?
   9 Thank you. It was excellent.
   10 Thank you. Enjoy the rest of your stay.

General vocabulary: Food and drink
2 1 We have to look at the menu first!
   2 No, thanks, I think I'll go straight to the main course.
   3 Can we see the wine list, please?
   4 We'd also like some water, please: one bottle of still *or* sparkling and one of sparkling *or* still, please.
   5 The main course is served with a selection of vegetables – potatoes, carrots and courgettes.
   6 I'm a vegetarian.
   7 I'll have chicken and a green salad, please.
   8 Would you like to finish with cheese or a dessert?

Unit 19

Grammar: *Should* and *have to*

1 1 You have to be at work by 8.30.
2 You don't have to have lunch in the canteen.
3 You shouldn't use so much paper.
4 You have to wear a suit and tie when you meet clients.
5 You should meet the new Human Resources director.
6 You have to leave before 6 if you want to catch your plane.
7 You shouldn't go to Paris next week.
8 You should leave work early during the school holidays.
9 You have to finish the report.
10 You don't have to get up early on Saturday.

2 1 Does he have to change planes in Singapore?
2 Should they be out so late?
3 Do they have to bring all the papers?
4 Should we talk to them more?
5 Do they have to work harder?

Pronunciation: Word stress

3

	Number of syllables	Stressed syllable
syllable	3	1st
organisation	5	4th
fantastic	3	2nd
vegetable	3	1st
photographer	4	2nd

Unit 20

Work vocabulary: Computers and the Internet

1 1 switch on your computer
2 log on
3 enter your password
4 connect to the Internet
5 open your emails
6 send your replies
7 disconnect from the Internet
8 switch off

2 1 e   2 d   3 f   4 g   5 h   6 a   7 c   8 b

Professional communication: Arranging meetings by phone

3 have a meeting – hold a meeting
cancel a meeting – not have a meeting
postpone a meeting – put back a meeting
fix a meeting – arrange a meeting
take part in a meeting – be at a meeting

4 Open the call   'Hello Regina, it's Guy. How are you?'
Ask for a meeting   'Guy, can we have a meeting soon?'
The reason   'We need to discuss the new computer network.'
The date   'How about next Thursday, the 17th?'
The time   '11 o'clock would be good for me.'
Agree   '11 o'clock no good? How about 12? OK? Fine.'
The place   'I can come to your office if you like.'
Ask for confirmation 'Can you send me these details by email, please?'

UNIT 21

General communication: Staying at hotels

1 1 I'd like one double room for my wife and myself, please.
 2 Please could you be out of your room by 10.30 on the morning you
  check out.
 3 You can ask for your bill in reception when you leave.
 4 Would you like an aperitif before your meal, madam?
 5 And what would you like to drink with your meal, sir?
 6 I'll have the soup as a starter and then chicken, please.
 7 How much is a room? Does that include everything?
 8 Would you order a taxi for me, please?

General vocabulary: Hotels

2 1 Have a drink   in the bar
  2 Eat a meal   in the dining room
  3 Pay your bill   in reception
  4 Park your car   in the garage
  5 Order a meal for your room from room service
  6 Take some exercise   in the gym
  7 Leave if there's a fire   through an emergency exit
  8 Go up to your room   in the lift / elevator
  9 Sit and read your newspaper in the lounge
 10 Sleep   in your bedroom

3 1 The wine waiter   brings you your drinks in the restaurant
   2 The guest   pays to stay in the hotel
   3 The porter   carries your bag to your room
   4 The receptionist   checks you in when you arrive
   5 The waiter   serves your meals
   6 The manager   looks after the staff
   7 The chambermaid   makes your bed and cleans your room
   8 The doorman   opens the door of your taxi

Unit 22

Grammar: *Many* and *much*

1 1 How many people work at the hospital?
   2 How many staff does the hospital employ?
   3 How much time did it take?
   4 How many hours did it take?
   5 How much holiday do you plan to take this year?
   6 How many weeks' holiday do you plan to take this year?
   7 How much furniture is there in your office?
   8 How many desks are there in your office?

Grammar: *A few* and *a little*

2 1 His company only has a few employees.
   2 I only have a little time left.
   3 I can only give you a little news about the situation.
   4 He usually drinks just a little wine because it makes him feel ill.
   5 We think there will be a little rain this evening.
   6 I'm sure she'll arrive in a few minutes.
   7 It will cost a little money to repair all the equipment.
   8 I want to give you a few words of advice.

3 1 c   2 d   3 b   4 b   5 d

Unit 23

Work vocabulary: Money and finance

1 1 planning   2 borrowing   3 saving   4 paying
   5 invoicing   6 investing
2 1 We sell pounds at a rate of 65 pence per euro.
   2 The bank says it will not lend us another million dollars.
   3 Every year we increase our prices.
   4 I have decided to save 10% of my income this year.

Professional communication: Helping visitors

3 1 Your visitor can't find her passport. – Where did you last see it?

2 Her suitcase got lost in transit. – I'll call the airline.

3 She has another appointment in one hour at another company. – I'll tell Mr Smith that you'd like to leave in half an hour.

4 She doesn't know how to get to her next appointment. – I'll book you a taxi.

5 She is late and the person she wants to meet is in another meeting. – I'm afraid Mr Jones is in a meeting now. I'll tell him you're here.

Unit 24

General communication: Money for shopping and travel

1 1 Where can I change some money?

2 Do you charge commission?

3 Can you tell me where the nearest cash point is?

4 What is the rate of exchange?

5 Do you accept credit cards?

6 Can you give me a receipt?

7 Can you change a two hundred euro note?

General vocabulary: Money

2 1 coins   2 notes   3 bank card

4 cash machine   5 cheque   6 cheque book

3 1 I think you should open a bank account.

2 Your employer can pay the money into your account at the end of every month.

3 You can take money from the account when you want.

4 Every month the bank sends you a bank statement.

5 This tells you how much money there is in the account.

6 If you want to save money, you can have a savings account.

7 The money in your savings account can earn interest of 2 or 3 per cent, depending on the currrent rates.

8 When you want to pay for things, you can write a cheque.

9 Or you can use your bank card.

10 You can also use your bank card to get money from a cash machine when the banks are closed.

Unit 25

Grammar: Present continuous for future plans

1 1 is going   2 is meeting   3 is attending   4 is staying
5 is opening   6 is playing   7 is having

2 1 am meeting / 'm meeting *or* am seeing / 'm seeing
2 am going / 'm going
3 am seeing / 'm seeing *or* am meeting / 'm meeting
4 are arriving
5 am having / 'm having
6 am not doing / 'm not doing

Unit 26

Work vocabulary: Solving problems

1 1 We have a major technical problem with the computer network.
2 We have to find a solution quickly.
3 I'm sure our technical staff can solve the problem.
4 If the problem continues, our customers will complain.

2 1 a difficult colleague   2 time   3 organisation   4 understaffing
5 quality   6 work environment   7 slow payers   8 stress
9 customer service

Professional communication: Solving problems by phone

3 1 How can I help you?
2 What exactly is the problem?
3 There must be an answer to this problem.
4 We can find a solution to this.
5 I'll see what I can do.
6 Why don't you try switching it off and on again?

Unit 27

General communication: Making invitations

1 1 Would you like to come to dinner on Saturday night? (a)
2 Can you come to the cinema next week? (a)
3 Are you free on Friday evening? We're having a party. (b)
4 How about a game of tennis at the weekend? (b)

General vocabulary: Health and fitness

2 1 HEART
2 EXERCISE
3 FAT
4 SLEEP
5 DIET
6 FRESH

7 LAZY
8 LOSE
9 SLIM/THIN
10 GIVE
11 LIVE
12 UNHEALTHY
13 WEIGHT

Unit 28

Grammar: Present perfect

1 1 I have been to almost every country in the world.
2 I have bought hundreds of companies in the US and Europe.
3 I have learnt/learned how to fly a jumbo jet.
4 I have met the Presidents of both the USA and China.
5 He has never spoken to the US President.
6 He has never sat in the pilot's seat of a jumbo jet.
7 He has never visited Japan, China or Russia.
8 He has never owned a company.

2 1 Have you met Sophie? No, I haven't. Nice to meet you
2 Have you seen our brochure? Yes, I have. It's very good.
3 Have you ever bought any of our products? No. Not yet!
4 Have you ever been to the USA? Yes. I've been there twice.
5 Have you had lunch yet? No, not yet. Have you?

3 1 have received 2 have ordered 3 have also agreed
4 Have they ever bought 5 We have never sold

Unit 29

Work vocabulary: Trends

1 1 When *Whammo* magazine was launched, sales rose / increased to
12,000 copies a week in the first year.
2 Sales also went up a lot in year 2.
3 But year 3 was not so good and they increased only a little.
4 In year 4 they went up by just 2,000 copies.
5 And sales stayed the same in year 5.
6 In year 6 they fell for the first time, to 24,000 copies.
7 But there was an increase again in year 7.
8 This year, with more money for advertising, the target is to reach
sales of 30,000 copies for the first time.

Professional communication: Arranging meetings by email

2 1 fix 2 holiday 3 free 4 convenient 5 busy
6 make 7 let's 8 meet 9 forward 10 agenda

General vocabulary: Lifestyles

1 1 e   2 g   3 f   4 c   5 d   6 a   7 b

General vocabulary: Learning vocabulary

2

Verb	Person noun	General noun
organise	organiser	organisation
manage	manager	management
produce	producer	production
compete	competitor	competition
decide	decision-maker	decision
invest	investor	investment

General communication: Saying goodbye

3   1 See you again in the autumn.

2 Give my best wishes to Jim.

3 We're looking forward to the next meeting.

4 Until we meet again.

5 Drive safely.

6 Say hello to Cynthia from me.

7 Thanks for your hospitality.

8 It was so good of you to invite us.

9 Have a safe journey.

10 Ring us when you get back.

English365

Personal Study Book 1
Audio CD

Contents of the Audio CD

Introduction

Welcome to the *English365* Personal Study Book 1 Audio CD.
There are three parts to the CD:

- Part 1 contains **Listening exercises** to help you practise
  your English on your own. The exercises practise basic
  work like the alphabet, numbers, dates and
  measurements. They are all very important to remember.
  We hope you find them useful.

- Part 2 contains the **Pronunciation** work from the
  English365 Student's Book.

- Part 3 contains the **Social English dialogues** from the
  English365 Student's Book.

You will need to use the pause button when you listen to the CD.
Practise repeating what you hear as much as possible.

Part 1: Use the pause button to do the exercises.

Part 2: Repeating what you hear will help you to improve your
pronunciation.

Part 3: Repeating what you hear will help you to remember important
Social English phrases.

Part 1 Listening units

There are 12 Listening units in this part. For each unit there is:

- Practice   Listen to the CD and repeat. Look at the book too if you need to. If this part is easy for you, go straight on to the exercise.
- Exercise   Listen to the CD and write your answers in the book. Then look at the Answer key (page 91) to check your answers.
- Over to you   Listen to Sally Donaldson talking about the same subject. If you want, read what she says in the book too. Then you can answer the same questions.

1 The alphabet

Sally Donaldson

PRACTICE

Listen and practise saying the letters of the alphabet in English:

A – B – C – D – E – F – G – H – I – J – K – L – M – N – O – P – Q – R – S – T – U – V – W – X – Y – Z

You can say 'double oh' in 'Liverpool': L-I-V-E-R-P-double oh –L.
You can say 'Next word' before you start a new word.

EXERCISE

Spell the names of these places:

1   ....
2   ....
3   ....
4   ....
5   ....
6   ....

OVER TO YOU

Now listen to Sally:

INTERVIEWER: Sally, how do you spell your name?

SALLY: My name's Sally Donaldson. That's S–A–double L–Y, next word D–O–N–A–L–D–S–O–N.

INTERVIEWER: And who do you work for?

SALLY: I work for the Open University. Shall I spell that?

INTERVIEWER: No, that's OK, thanks. And where do you work?

SALLY: I work in Milton Keynes. That's two words: M–I–L–T–O–N, next word K–E–Y–N–E–S.

Now answer the same questions:
How do you spell your name?
Who do you work for? How do you spell it?
Where do you work? How do you spell it?

2 Numbers

PRACTICE

Listen and practise saying numbers in English:

1	one	18	eighteen
2	two	19	nineteen
3	three	20	twenty
4	four	21	twenty-one
5	five	30	thirty
6	six	40	forty
7	seven	50	fifty
8	eight	60	sixty
9	nine	70	seventy
10	ten	80	eighty
11	eleven	90	ninety
12	twelve	100	a hundred / one hundred
13	thirteen	101	a hundred and one
14	fourteen	1,000	a thousand
15	fifteen	10,000	ten thousand
16	sixteen	1,000,000	a million
17	seventeen		

0 is usually pronounced 'oh' or 'zero'.

We say telephone numbers like this:
00 33 1 42 64 97 55 = double oh – double three – one – four two – six four – nine seven – double five

Years are like this:
1715 = seventeen fifteen   1974 = nineteen seventy-four
2003 = two thousand and three

And money:
€10 = ten euros $20 = twenty dollars   £10.50 = ten pounds fifty

How do we say these numbers?

1 Standard numbers:
   14   57   98   104   369   1,250   6,000,000
2 Telephone numbers:
   00 44 1904 659723   00 33 1 42 56 89 77
3 Years:
   1854   1996   2001
4 Money:
   £100 $10,000   €560   £4.50   €7.83

Listen to Sally:

INTERVIEWER: How old are you, Sally?
      SALLY: I'm 32.
INTERVIEWER: When did you start working for the Open University?
      SALLY: In 2002.
INTERVIEWER: What's your work telephone number?
      SALLY: It's 01908 369255.
INTERVIEWER: And what's your favourite number?
      SALLY: My favourite number is 3.

Now answer the same questions:
How old are you?
When did you start working for your organisation?
What's your work telephone number?
And what's your favourite number?

3 Days of the week

Listen and practise saying the days of the week:
Monday – Tuesday – Wednesday – Thursday – Friday – Saturday – Sunday

EXERCISE

Look at Bill's diary for next week and answer the questions.

1 When is Bill flying to New York?

....

2 When is he flying back?

....

3 When is he having lunch with Toni?

....

4 When is he seeing Amanda?

....

5 When is he seeing the bank manager?

....

6 When is he meeting the new boss?

....

7 When is he sleeping late?

....

Day	
M	See bank manager
T	Have lunch with Toni
W	Meet the new boss
T	Fly to New York
F	Discuss figures with Amanda
S	Fly back from New York
S	Sleep late!

OVER TO YOU

Listen to Sally:

INTERVIEWER: What day is it today?

SALLY: It's Wednesday today.

INTERVIEWER: What's your favourite day? Why?

SALLY: My favourite day is Sunday because it's the only day when I don't have to get up early.

Now answer the same questions:
What day is it today?
What's your favourite day? Why?

4 Months of the year

PRACTICE

Listen and practise saying the months of the year:
January – February – March – April – May – June – July – August – September – October – November – December

Look at the national calendar and answer the questions.

1 When do they have their National Day?

    ....

2 When do they have their Independence Day?

    ....

3 When do they have their Children's Day?

    ....

4 When do they have their Mothers' Day?

    ....

5 When do they have their Winter Holiday?

    ....

6 When do they have their Summer Holiday?

    ....

Month	
J	New Year's Day
F	Winter Holiday
M	Mothers' Day
A	Spring Holiday
M	National Day
J	Fathers' Day
J	President's Birthday
A	Summer Holiday
S	Independence Day
O	Autumn Holiday
N	Children's Day
D	Christmas Day

Listen to Sally:

INTERVIEWER: When do you have your summer holiday, Sally?

SALLY: We usually have our big holiday of the year in July or August.

INTERVIEWER: And do you take any other holidays?

SALLY: Yes, we always go skiing in February.

Now answer the same questions:

When do you have your summer holiday?

Do you take any other holidays?

5 Dates

Listen and practise saying the numbers we use to say the date:

1st	first	6th	sixth
2nd	second	7th	seventh
3rd	third	20th	twentieth
4th	fourth	21st	twenty-first
5th	fifth	30th	thirtieth

In British English we say the date like this:

Monday the first of February *or* Monday February the first

In American English we say:

Tuesday twenty-second March *or* Tuesday March twenty-second

Match the dates of birth with the people, then answer the questions.

George Washington	18 May 1920
Michelangelo Buonarotti	22 February 1732
Pope John Paul II	29 September 1547
Napoleon Bonaparte	6 March 1475
Miguel de Cervantes	15 August 1769

1 When was George Washington born?   ....
2 When was Michelangelo Buonarotti born?   ....
3 When was Pope John Paul II born?   ....
4 When was Napoleon Bonaparte born?   ....
5 When was Miguel de Cervantes born?   ....

OVER TO YOU

Listen to Sally:

INTERVIEWER: When's your birthday, Sally?
SALLY: It's the twentieth of May.
INTERVIEWER: And do you have any other important dates in your life?
SALLY: Well, my husband's birthday is the fifth of December and our wedding anniversary is the third of April.

Now answer the same questions:
When's your birthday?
Do you have any other important dates in your life? What are they?

6 The time

PRACTICE

Listen and practise saying the time in two different ways:

one oh five	five past one
two ten	ten past two
three fifteen	a quarter past three
four twenty	twenty past four
five twenty-five	twenty-five past five
six thirty	half past six
seven thirty-five	twenty-five to eight
eight forty	twenty to nine
nine forty-five	a quarter to ten
ten fifty	ten to eleven
eleven fifty-five	five to twelve
twelve o'clock midday	twelve o'clock midnight

'am' means IN the morning (before 12 o'clock midday)
'pm' means IN the afternoon, in the evening, or AT night (after 12 o'clock midday)

What's the time? Say each of the times in two different ways.

1   am   2   pm   3   am

....
....

                  ....
....

....
....

4   pm   5   pm   6   pm

....
....

....
....

....
....

OVER TO YOU

Listen to Sally:

INTERVIEWER: What time do you get up in the morning?

SALLY: Between seven and seven fifteen in the week and about midday on Sunday!

INTERVIEWER: What time do you have lunch?

SALLY: Usually at about twelve thirty.

INTERVIEWER: What time do you go to bed at night?

SALLY: Eleven to eleven thirty in the week but much later at the weekend!

Now answer the same questions:

What time do you get up in the morning?

What time do you have lunch?

What time do you go to bed at night?

7 Measurements

PRACTICE

Listen and practise saying these dimensions:

Adjectives	Nouns
My office is five metres long.	It has a length of five metres.
It's three metres wide.	It has a width of three metres.
It's two metres high.	It has a height of two metres.

Our swimming pool is ten metres long. It has a length of ten metres.
It's four metres wide. It has a width of four metres.
It's one metre deep. It has a depth of one metre.

EXERCISE

Look at the picture of the swimming pool and answer the questions using adjectives:

1 How long is the pool? ....
2 How wide is it? ....
3 How deep is it? ....

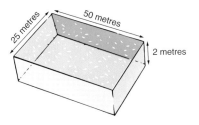

Now answer the same questions using nouns:

4 How long is the pool? ....
5 How wide is it? ....
6 How deep is it? ....

Look at the picture of the meeting room and answer the questions using adjectives:

7 How long is the room? ....
8 How wide is it? ....
9 How high is it? ....

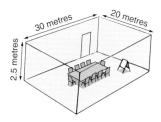

Now answer the same questions using nouns:

10 How long is the room? ....
11 How wide is it? ....
12 How high is it? ....

OVER TO YOU

Listen to Sally:

INTERVIEWER: Sally, do you have a big office? How big is it?
SALLY: Actually, I work in an open plan office with about 50 other people. I guess it's about 30 metres long, and about 20 metres wide.
INTERVIEWER: And is it high? How high is it?
SALLY: Yes, there's quite a lot of space. It's about 4 metres high.
INTERVIEWER: And what about where you live? Do you have a big room at home where you can relax? How big is it?
SALLY: Yes, we have a lounge where we talk and watch TV. I guess it's about 6 metres long and about 5 metres wide.

Now answer the same questions:
How big is the place where you work? How high is it?
Do you have a big room at home where you can relax? How big is it?

8 Countries and nationalities

PRACTICE

Listen and practise saying the names of the world's main continents:

We usually make the names of nationalities by adding:

-ish	as in	Danish (someone from Denmark)
-ese	as in	Japanese (someone from Japan)
-n, -an or *-ian*	as in	Russian (someone from Russia)
-i	as in	Saudi (someone from Saudi Arabia)

But not all nationalities are formed from countries like this. For example, someone from *France* is *French*.

EXERCISE

Can you say the nationalities of these people? Finish the sentences:

1 Manuela is from Italy. She's ....
2 Placido is from Spain. He's ....
3 Mercedes is from Portugal. She's ....
4 Anne Marie is from Sweden. She's ....
5 Magda is from Poland. She's ....
6 Domenika is from Hungary. She's ....
7 Elisabeth is from the USA. She's ....
8 Bill is from Great Britain. He's ....
9 Huang is from China. He's ....
10 Anna Greta is from Norway. She's ....
11 Sylvie is from Holland. She's ....
12 Jean is from Belgium. He's ....

Listen to Sally:

INTERVIEWER: Sally, where are you from. What's your nationality?

SALLY: I'm British.

INTERVIEWER: And all your family too?

SALLY: No, my mother is Irish, and my husband is Russian.

INTERVIEWER: And if you could choose another nationality, what would you choose to be?

SALLY: I think I'd choose to be . . . maybe Japanese.

INTERVIEWER: Why?

SALLY: Because I love the country, I love the people, and I love their design and their sense of style.

Now answer the same questions:
Where are you from? What's your nationality?
And all your family too?
If you could choose another nationality, what would you choose to be?
Why?

9 Daily routines

PRACTICE

Listen and practise talking about Maria's daily routine:
She wakes up at six thirty / half past six.
She has a shower at six forty / twenty to seven.
She has breakfast at seven o'clock.
She leaves home at seven thirty / half past seven.
She gets to work at eight o'clock.
She has a cup of coffee at eight ten / ten past eight.
She goes to the daily departmental meeting at nine o'clock.
She works on her computer at nine thirty / half past nine.
She has a meeting with a client at eleven o'clock.
She has lunch at twelve o'clock.
She reads the company magazine at one o'clock.
She makes some telephone calls at one thirty / half past one.
She goes to the factory at two thirty / half past two.
She leaves the office at five o'clock.
She gets home at five thirty / half past five.
She has dinner at seven o'clock.
She watches the news on TV at eight o'clock.
She goes to bed at eleven thirty / half past eleven.

EXERCISE

Now answer these questions:

1 What does she do at 6.30? ....
2 What does she do at 7 o'clock? ....
3 What does she do at 8 o'clock? ....
4 What does she do at 9 o'clock? ....
5 What does she do at 11 o'clock? ....
6 What does she do at 12 o'clock? ....
7 What does she do at 1 o'clock? ....
8 What does she do at 5 o'clock? ....
9 What does she do at 7 o'clock
   in the evening? ....

OVER TO YOU

Listen to Sally:

INTERVIEWER: Sally, tell us about your daily routine. What do you do every morning before you go to work?

SALLY: I always start the day with a very hot shower and then I have a cup of strong black coffee for breakfast.

INTERVIEWER: And how do you get to work?

SALLY: I drive. It takes about 15 minutes if the traffic is not too bad.

INTERVIEWER: And what do you do when you get to work?

SALLY: First I check my emails and then I plan the day with the two people I work with.

INTERVIEWER: And in the afternoon?

SALLY: I usually have a meeting in the afternoon and I also work on reports.

INTERVIEWER: And in the evening?

SALLY: It depends. We usually eat around 7.30 and then watch TV or see friends. But we go to the gym two or three nights a week and we go to the cinema quite often too.

Now answer the same questions:

What do you do every morning before you go to work?

How do you get to work?

What do you do when you get to work?

What do you do in the afternoon?

What do you do in the evening?

10 Communicating at work 1: Meeting people

PRACTICE

Listen and practise saying these phrases to talk about yourself.

Hello. My name's .... (*your name*)

I'm a / the .... (*your job*) with .... (*your organisation*)

We make / we provide .... (*your organisation's activity*)

I work in .... (*the place where you work*)

I work in the .... Department.

EXERCISE

What questions do you ask to get information about someone's:

1 name? ....

2 country? ....

3 organisation? ....

4 job? ....

5 location? ....

6 family? ....

7 free time? ....

OVER TO YOU

Listen to Sally:

INTERVIEWER: Sally, where do you come from?

SALLY: I'm from Manchester originally.

INTERVIEWER: Who do you work for?

SALLY: The Open University.

INTERVIEWER: What do you do?

SALLY: I'm a course administrator.

INTERVIEWER: Where do you work?

SALLY: In Milton Keynes, it's about 40 kilometres from London.

INTERVIEWER: Are you married?

SALLY: Yes. My husband's a musician.

INTERVIEWER: What do you do in your free time?

SALLY: I relax! I like reading, seeing friends, cinema, keeping fit . . . that kind of thing.

Now answer the same questions:

Where do you come from?

Who do you work for?

What do you do?

Where do you work?

Are you married?

What do you do in your free time?

11 Communicating at work 2: Dealing with visitors

PRACTICE

Listen and practise saying phrases you can use with visitors to your organisation:

Hello, nice to meet you.
Hello, how are you?
Did you have a good trip?
Can I take your bag?
How's the weather in Tokyo?

EXERCISE

Complete the sentences which you can use to greet visitors to your organisation:

1 What's your .... ?
2 Do you have an identity .... ?
3 Please take a ....
4 Mrs Smith's office is on the tenth ....
5 It's OK. We can take the ....
6 Would you like .... ?

OVER TO YOU

Listen to Sally:

INTERVIEWER: Sally, do you get a lot of visitors in your job?
SALLY: Yes, quite a lot. About once a week. Usually from other European countries.
INTERVIEWER: And what do you say to them? What's the first thing you say?
SALLY: I say: 'Hello, my name's Sally Donaldson. Welcome to the Open University.'
INTERVIEWER: And what do you say to make them feel at home?
SALLY: I say something like: 'Is everything OK?' and 'If you have any problems or questions, just let me know.'

Now answer the same questions:

Do you get a lot of visitors in your job?
What do you say to them? What's the first thing you say?
And what do you say to make them feel at home?

12 Communicating at work 3: Telephoning

PRACTICE

Listen and practise saying these basic telephone phrases:

A: Hello. This is Martine Dufour. Can I help you?
B: Good morning. My name's Andreas Kunz. Can I speak to Brendan Richards, please?
A: I'm sorry. He's busy at the moment.

B: Can you ask him to call me back, please?
A: Yes. Can you give me your number, please?
B: Yes. It's 00 44 1271 458752.
A: OK. I'll tell him. Thank you for calling.
B: Thank you. Goodbye.

EXERCISE

Complete the sentences which you can use on the telephone:

1 Taking phone messages:
   I'm sorry. She's not in the .... today.
   Can I give her a .... ?
   No, thanks. I'll call back this ....
   Please can you give me your name and .... ?
2 Arranging meetings by phone:
   When do you want to .... ?
   I'll look in my ....
3 Solving problems:
   Hello. I have a problem. Can you .... ?
   OK, I'll check this and call you back in half an ....
   Fine. Thanks. Speak to you ....

OVER TO YOU

Listen to Sally:

INTERVIEWER: Sally, how do you answer the phone when someone calls you?
SALLY: I usually just say 'Sally Donaldson' or sometimes I say 'Sally Donaldson speaking.'
INTERVIEWER: And what do you say if you have to take a message?
SALLY: Something like 'Can I give her a message?' or 'Would you like me to give her a message?'
INTERVIEWER: And if you have to arrange a meeting by phone?
SALLY: I would say something like 'Can we meet on Friday?' or 'Are you free next week?'
INTERVIEWER: What's your golden rule for telephoning?
SALLY: I always make sure I have all the information I need for the call in front of me before I call. It's terrible if you have to start running around looking for things while you're on the phone.

Now answer the same questions:
How do you answer the phone when someone calls you?
What do you say if you have to take a message?
What do you say if you have to arrange a meeting by phone?
What's your golden rule for telephoning?

Part 2 Pronunciation

In this part, you can listen again to the pronunciation work in the type 1 units in the *English365* Student's Book 1 and practise repeating key phrases.

1 Reply questions (see Student's Book Unit 1)

Listen to Susie pronounce the you in this conversation. When you do this, it's important to stress the you in the question:

MARIA: What do you do exactly?
SUSIE: We make inline skates. And **you**? What do **you** do?
MARIA: We sell bicycles.

Now practise repeating what Susie says.

2 The present simple third person (see Student's Book Unit 4)

Listen to the three ways in which we pronounce the third person -s in the present simple:

/s/ gets   /z/ goes   /ɪz/ watches

Now listen to these verbs and repeat:

leaves   writes   relaxes   sells   works   buys
organises   meets   visits   listens   manages   does

3 Linking (see Student's Book Unit 7)

In normal speech, we usually connect final consonant sounds to following vowels. Practise saying these sentences with linked sounds:

1 Telenor is a big company.
2 It's a very big building.
3 I think it's very, very flexible.
4 There's a big fitness centre, which is very good.
5 Yes, I like it a lot.

4 Weak stress 1 (see Student's Book Unit 10)

We pronounce some words and syllables with strong stress, others with weak stress. Listen for the weak stress in these sentences and then repeat:

1 Polite? We're politer than the rest.
2 Fast? We're faster than the rest.
3 Cheap? We're less expensive than the rest.
4 Big? We're the biggest in the world.
5 Good? We're the best in the world.

5 Past simple verbs (see Student's Book Unit 13)

Listen to the three different ways we pronounce -ed:

/ɪd/ wanted   /t/ walked   /d/ played

Listen to the pronunciation of these verbs and repeat:

liked   decreased   decided   looked   wanted   increased
enjoyed   talked   received   listened   walked   visited

Pronounce the past form of these irregular verbs:

bring – brought   buy – bought   read – read   say – said   see – saw
speak – spoke   take – took   tell – told   think – thought

6 Sentence stress (see Student's Book Unit 16)

In English we stress the words in sentences which are important to communicate our ideas. Stressed words are spoken with more power and sound than unstressed words. Listen to this conversation, paying attention to the stressed words:

A: Are you working from home next week?
B: Yes, I'm working from home to the end of the month.
A: Are you busy?
B: Yes, but I'm enjoying the work.

Now listen again and repeat each sentence in the conversation.

7 Word stress (see Student's Book Unit 19)

When we pronounce words with more than one syllable, we stress one syllable more than the others. Listen to the example:

China   Chinese

Listen to these sentences and repeat them with the same stress:

1 Yeah, it was a fantastic time …
2 It's a very dynamic place …
3 With a traditional person …
4 People are very open about money …
5 Hong Kong is a very fashionable place …
6 … I think family is very important …
7 … modern houses and flats …
8 … ten or fifteen per cent …

8 Saying numbers and prices (see Student's Book Unit 22)

Listen and repeat these numbers and prices:

Numbers
twenty-five
a hundred *or* one hundred
a hundred and one *or* one hundred and one
a thousand *or* one thousand
two thousand and one
ten thousand five hundred and fifty
five hundred thousand
a million *or* one million
a billion *or* one billion

Prices
fifty p
four pounds ninety-nine p *or* four pounds ninety-nine
two hundred and fifty pounds
a hundred and fifty thousand euros *or* one hundred
    and fifty thousand euros
a hundred and fifty million pounds *or* one hundred
    and fifty million pounds
ninety-nine cents
four dollars ninety-five cents *or* four dollars ninety-five
two thousand five hundred dollars
two point five million dollars *or* two and a half million dollars

9 Weak stress 2 (see Student's Book Unit 25)

Unstressed words are pronounced with the schwa /ə/. Using the schwa correctly is very important for your understanding and pronunciation. Listen to the questions and answers in this conversation:

A: What are you doing next week?
B: I'm going to Poland.
A: Poland? What are you doing there?
B: I'm visiting a friend.
A: How long are you staying?
B: Just for a few days.
A: When are you coming back?
B: Next Friday.
A: Are you doing anything at the weekend?
B: Yes, I'm going camping.

Now listen again and repeat each sentence.

10 Spelling and pronunciation (see Student's Book Unit 28)

It is sometimes difficult to know how to pronounce words as the spelling doesn't always help you. Here are ten easily mispronounced words which have come up in this course. Listen and repeat each one:

colleague   jewellery   aisle   castle   talked
weight   impatient   dessert   budget   salmon

Part 3 Social English dialogues

In this part, you can listen again to the dialogues from the type 3 units in Student's Book 1 and practise repeating key phrases.

1 It's almost the weekend

Listen to people talking about what they plan to do at the weekend and then practise saying the key phrases (see Student's Book Unit 3):

Arriving at the office on Friday
A: Hi, John.
B: Morning. How are you?
A: Fine, thanks. And you?
B: Not bad. A bit tired.
A: Never mind. It's almost the weekend.

Going for lunch
A: Ready for some lunch?
B: Yes, good idea.
A: Where do you want to eat?
B: Shall we eat out?
A: Yes, it's Friday. The new Italian place?
B: Great. Let's go.

A weekend away
A: Do you have any plans for the weekend?
B: I'm going to visit my brother.
A: Where does he live?
B: In Stratford-upon-Avon.
A: Stratford? It's a lovely place. Have a good time!
B: Thanks. I will!

Going home
A: I'm going. See you next week.
B: OK, see you.
A: Have a good weekend.
B: Thanks. You too. Bye.

2 Shopping

Listen to people talking about shopping and then practise saying the key phrases (see Student's Book Unit 6):

Looking around
A: Hello, can I help you?
B: No, it's OK thanks. I'm just looking.
A: OK. Just ask me if you need some help.

Asking for help

B: Could I try this on, please?

A: Yes, of course. The changing rooms are just there.

B: Thank you.

A: (*A few minutes later*) So, how's that?

B: I'm not sure. It's a bit small. Have you got it in a larger size?

A: No, I'm sorry, we haven't.

B: Oh, I see. I think I'll leave it then.

Asking about the price

B: Excuse me, how much is this, please?

A: It's 47 euros.

B: OK, I'll take it.

A: Fine. You can pay over there.

Asking about payment

A: That's 47 euros, please.

B: Thank you. Can I pay by credit card?

A: Yes, of course ... Sign here, please.

B: OK.

A: Here's your card and your receipt is in the bag. Thank you.

B: Thank you. Goodbye.

3 Getting around

Listen to people talking about getting around a city they don't know, and then practise saying the key phrases (see Student's Book Unit 9):

Buying a ticket

A: Hi. Three tickets for the Wendella Lake tour, please. Two adults and one child.

B: That's $22.50, please.

A: Thanks. What time does the next ferry leave, please?

B: At 3 o'clock, in 25 minutes.

A: OK. Thanks.

Taking the train

A: Excuse me. Does this go to O'Hare Airport?

B: No. You need to take the blue line.

A: OK, so where do I go?

B: Go to Lake Street and transfer to the blue line and then take it to the end of the line.

A: Great. Thanks for your help.

Catching a bus

A: Excuse me. Can I get a bus to the Magnificent Mile from here?

B: Yes, you want a number 151 or a 147. Or you can take a cab or walk.

A: When's the next bus?

B: Ten minutes. But they're not always on time.

A: Thanks.

Getting a cab

A: How much is that?
B: That's $10.20.
A: Here you are, $12.00. Keep the change.
B: Thank you.
A: Could I have a receipt?
B: Sure. Here you go. Have a good day.

4 I've got news for you

Listen to people responding to news and then practise saying the key phrases (see Student's Book Unit 12):

Responding to good news

A: Hi. Good weekend?
B: Yes, very. I have some news. My wife's pregnant.
A: Wonderful. Congratulations!
B: Thanks. We're very happy.
A: Oh, good. We must celebrate.

Responding to interesting news

A: Hey, Peter. I've got an email from China.
B: Really?
A: Yes, it's a new customer, I think. They want information about our products.
B: Great. Please tell me if you hear any more from them.
A: Of course I will.

Responding to bad news

A: So you leave for the US tonight?
B: Don't ask! My trip's cancelled!
A: Why's that?
B: Because I have to stay here for a meeting with my boss.
A: Oh, well, never mind. Now you can come to Helen's party tonight.

Responding to surprising news

A: See you tomorrow.
B: Yeah, see you. What are you doing tonight?
A: I'm not sure yet. I might go jogging.
B: You're joking! I don't believe it. You hate sport.
A: Yes, but I need the exercise.

5 Getting there

Listen to people talking about travelling by plane, and then practise saying the key phrases (see Student's Book Unit 15):

Checking in

A: Can I check in here for Vienna?
B: Yes. Can I see your passport and ticket, please?

A: Of course.

B: Would you prefer a window or an aisle seat?

A: An aisle seat, please.

B: Boarding is at 17.30 at gate 45.

Getting information at the gate

A: Excuse me, do you have any information about the Amsterdam flight?

B: Yes, the flight is delayed by 45 minutes.

A: OK, so when is boarding?

B: Boarding is now at 18.30. I'm very sorry for the delay.

On the plane

A: Excuse me, could you put your bag in the overhead locker?

B: They're full. There's no room.

A: Can you put it under your seat?

B: OK, I'll do that.

A: Thank you.

Arriving without luggage

A: Hello, my suitcase didn't arrive.

B: Right, I need some information from you.

A: OK, this is my flight information and a local address.

B: Thank you. You're very organised.

A: Yes, this isn't the first time!

6 Restaurant talk

Listen to people talking in a restaurant and then practise saying the key phrases (see Student's Book Unit 18):

At the restaurant

A: Good evening. I have a reservation. My name's Brillakis.

B: Yes, the table by the window. Can I take your coats?

A: Thank you.

C: Thanks.

B: So, the menu and the wine list. Would you like a drink before you order?

Before the meal

B: Are you ready to order?

C: Yes. We'll both have the pâté as a starter, please. What's John Dory?

B: John Dory is a kind of white sea fish.

C: Then I'll have the John Dory.

A: The salmon, please.

B: Right. And to drink?

A: We'll have a bottle of the house white.

During the meal

B: Is everything all right?

C: Yes, thanks. Oh, can I have some more bread, please?

B: Sure. And would you like some more wine?

A: No, thanks. Actually, could we have a bottle of sparkling mineral water?

After the meal

B: So, did you enjoy your meal?

C: Yes, thank you. It was very nice.

B: Good. And would you like anything else? More coffee?

C: No, thank you. Could we have the bill, please?

B: Of course.

7 Enjoy your stay

Listen to people talking in a hotel and then practise saying the key phrases (see Student's Book Unit 21):

Checking in

A: Hello, my name's Sanchez, I have a reservation.

B: Good evening. Yes, Mr Sanchez, a single room, for two nights.
Could you complete this form, please?

A: Of course.

B: Thank you. So, it's room 414, on the fourth floor. Do you need any help with your bags?

A: No, thanks. I can manage.

A morning call

A: Hello, can I have breakfast in my room, please? At 7 o'clock?

B: Certainly, sir.

A: So I'd like a wake-up call at 6.30. Can you do that?

B: That's fine. So, morning call at 6.30, breakfast at 7 o'clock.

A problem

A: Good morning. There's a problem with the shower. There's no hot water.
Can you send someone to look at it?

B: Of course, I'll send someone immediately. What's your room number?

A: 414.

B: Fine. Someone will be with you in a moment.

Leaving

A: Morning, can I check out, please? Room 414.

B: Right, Mr Sanchez. Anything from the minibar last night?

A: No, nothing.

B: OK, here's your bill. Sign here, please. Have a good trip home.

8 Money talk

Listen to people talking about money and then practise saying the key phrases (see Student's Book Unit 24):

Asking a colleague for money

A: Clare, I haven't got much cash on me.

B: Do you want to borrow some money?

A: Could you lend me ten pounds until tomorrow?

B: No problem.

A: Cheers. That's very nice of you.

Getting money out

A: Shall we find a restaurant?

B: Yes, but I need to get some money out first.

A: OK, I'll wait here.

B: Is there a cash point nearby?

A: Yes, there's a bank just across the road, over there.

Changing money

A: Hello, I'd like to change some euros into Swiss francs.

B: How much do you want to change?

A: What's the commission?

B: There's no commission if you change more than 200 euros.

A: OK, then I'll change 300, thanks.

Getting change

A: Excuse me, do you have any change?

B: What do you need?

A: I need some coins for the coffee machine.

B: Just a second, yes, here you are.

A: Thanks very much.

9 Inviting

Listen to people making invitations and then practise saying the key phrases (see Student's Book Unit 27):

Inviting someone

SUE: Vasili, I'd like to invite you to lunch tomorrow after our meeting.

VASILI: Oh, thank you very much.

SUE: There's a Mexican restaurant nearby. Is that OK for you?

VASILI: That sounds good.

SUE: Good. I'll reserve a table.

Saying 'maybe' to an invitation

SUE: We're having a little party at the weekend. Can you and Jitka come?

BERNDT: That sounds nice. Thank you. But I'll have to check with Jitka.

SUE: Fine. Can you let me know before Friday?

BERNDT: I'll let you know before then.

Saying 'no' to an invitation

SUE: Michel, I want to try the new vegetarian café across the road. Are you free for lunch on Friday?

MICHEL: I'm afraid I can't. I have some visitors from the US. But thanks for the invitation.

SUE: That's OK. Another time.

MICHEL: Definitely.

Cancelling an invitation

VASILI: I'm really sorry Sue, but I have to cancel lunch tomorrow. Something's come up.

SUE: No problem.

VASILI: Can we fix another time?

SUE: Let's do something next week.

VASILI: Yes, sorry about that.

10 Saying goodbye

Listen to people saying goodbye and then practise saying the key phrases (see Student's Book Unit 30):

Organising airport transport

A: Linda, when are you leaving?

B: I've ordered a taxi for 1 o'clock.

A: I'm leaving the office early. I can take you to the airport, if you want.

B: That's very kind but I can take a taxi. It's no problem.

Exchanging contact information

A: Here's my business card.

B: Oh, thanks, I'm afraid I don't have one with me.

A: Don't worry.

B: But this is my mobile number and email address.

A: Great. I'll contact you on Monday with the information you want.

Giving a present

A: Before you go, this is for you.

B: What's this?

A: It's a little present to say thank you.

B: It's beautiful. Thank you very much.

A: My pleasure. Thank you.

Saying goodbye

B: I have to go. The taxi's here.

A: Well, it was nice working with you.

B: Yes, the same for me. It was great.

A: Have a good trip back.

B: See you soon, I hope.

A: Take care. Bye.

Answer key to Listening units

1 The alphabet

1 S–A–N, next word: F–R–A–N–C–I–S–C–O
2 B–O–R–D–E–A–U–X
3 V–I–C–E–N–Z–A
4 J–O–H–A–N–N–E–S–B–U–R–G
5 R–I–O, next word D–E, next word J–A–N–E–I–R–O
6 H–I–R–O–S–H–I–M–A

2 Numbers

1 Standard numbers:

14	fourteen
57	fifty-seven
98	ninety-eight
104	a hundred and four
369	three hundred and sixty-nine
1,250	one thousand two hundred and fifty
6,000,000	six million

2 Telephone numbers:

00 44 1904 659723	double oh – double four – one nine oh four – six five nine – seven two three
00 33 1 42 56 89 77	double oh – double three – one – four two – five six – eight nine – double seven

3 Years:

1854	eighteen fifty-four
1996	nineteen ninety-six
2001	two thousand and one

4 Money:

£100	a hundred pounds
$10,000	ten thousand dollars
€560	five hundred and sixty euros
£4.50	four pounds fifty
€7.83	seven euros eighty-three cents

3 Days of the week

1 On Thursday
2 On Saturday
3 On Tuesday
4 On Friday
5 On Monday
6 On Wednesday
7 On Sunday

4 Months of the year
1 In May
2 In September
3 In November
4 In March
5 In February
6 In August

5 Dates
1 On the twenty-second of February seventeen thirty-two
2 On the sixth of March fourteen seventy-five
3 On the eighteenth of May nineteen twenty
4 On the fifteenth of August seventeen sixty-nine
5 On the twenty-ninth of September fifteen forty-seven

6 The time
1 one forty-five in the morning *or* a quarter to two
2 two thirty in the afternoon *or* half past two
3 four fifteen in the morning *or* a quarter past four
4 six thirty-five in the evening *or* twenty-five to seven
5 eight twenty-five at night *or* twenty-five past eight
6 nine fifty at night *or* ten to ten

7 Measurements
1 It's 50 metres long.
2 It's 25 metres wide.
3 It's 2 metres deep.
4 It has a length of 50 metres.
5 It has a width of 25 metres.
6 It has a depth of 2 metres.
7 It's 30 metres long.
8 It's 20 metres wide.
9 It's 2.5 metres high.
10 It has a length of 30 metres.
11 It has a width of 20 metres.
12 It has a height of 2.5 metres.

8 Countries and nationalities
1 Manuela is from Italy. She's Italian.
2 Placido is from Spain. He's Spanish.
3 Mercedes is from Portugal. She's Portuguese.
4 Anne Marie is from Sweden. She's Swedish.
5 Magda is from Poland. She's Polish.
6 Domenika is from Hungary. She's Hungarian.
7 Elisabeth is from the USA. She's American.
8 Bill is from Great Britain. He's British.
9 Huang is from China. He's Chinese.

10 Anna Greta is from Norway. She's Norwegian.
11 Sylvie is from Holland. She's Dutch.
12 Jean is from Belgium. He's Belgian.

9 Daily routines

1 She wakes up.
2 She has breakfast.
3 She gets to work.
4 She goes to the daily departmental meeting.
5 She has a meeting with a client.
6 She has lunch.
7 She reads the company magazine.
8 She leaves the office.
9 She has dinner.

10 Communicating at work 1: Meeting people

1 What's your name?
2 Where are you from? *or* Where do you come from?
3 Who do you work for?
4 What do you do?
5 Where do you work? *or* Where are you based?
6 Are you married? *or* Do you have a family? *or* Do you have any children?
7 What do you do in your free time?

11 Communicating at work 2: Dealing with visitors

1 What's your name?
2 Do you have an identity card?
3 Please take a seat.
4 Mrs Smith's office is on the tenth floor.
5 It's OK. We can take the lift.
6 Would you like a cup of tea? *or* Would you like a cup of coffee? *or* Would you like something to drink?

12 Communicating at work 3: Telephoning

1 Taking phone messages:
I'm sorry. She's not in the office today.
Can I give her a message?
No, thanks. I'll call back this afternoon.
Please can you give me your name and number?

2 Arranging meetings by phone:
When do you want to meet?
I'll look in my diary.

3 Solving problems:
Hello. I have a problem. Can you help?
OK, I'll check this and call you back in half an hour.
Fine. Thanks. Speak to you soon.

Track numbers

Thanks and acknowledgements

The authors would like to thank:

- Will Capel and Sally Searby of Cambridge University Press for their unflinching support from start to finish;
- Alison Silver for her eagle eye for detail, for her good sense and good cheer throughout the editorial and proofreading process;
- Ruth Carim for proofreading;
- James Richardson for producing the recordings at The Soundhouse Ltd, London;
- Hart McLeod for the design and page make-up;
- Sue Evans; Lorenza, Mathieu, Jérôme and Michael Flinders; and Lyn, Jude, Ruth and Neil Sweeney for their patience;
- colleagues and friends at York Associates and in the School of Management, Community and Communication at York St John College for their tolerance of authorial distraction;
- and Chris Capper of Cambridge University Press for his immeasurable contribution to the project. It is above all his huge efforts which have made it possible.

The authors and publishers would like to thank the following for permission to reproduce photographs:
p. 15 ©Goodshoot/Alamy
p. 18 ©Bill Bachmann/alamy.com
p. 24 ©Robert Preston/alamy.com
p. 25 ©Jackson Smith/alamy.com
p. 32 ©Popperfoto/alamy.com
p. 36 ©Brand X Pictures/alamy.com
p. 39 ©Dallas and John Heaton/alamy.com
p. 44 ©Popperfoto/alamy.com
p. 66 ©Rod Edwards/alamy.com

Illustrations:
Linda Combi: pages 7, 16, 19 and 22
Richard Deverall: pages 7, 27, 33, and 35
Tim Oliver: pages 17, 20, 21, 38, 43, 72, 73 and 74